THE STANDARD GUIDE TO
RAZORS

Roy Ritchie & Ron Stewart

COLLECTOR BOOKS
A Division of Schroeder Publishing Co., Inc.

The current values in this book should be used only as a guide. They are not intended to set prices, which vary from one section of the country to another. Auction prices as well as dealer prices vary greatly and are affected by condition as well as demand. Neither the Authors nor the Publisher assumes responsibility for any losses that might be incurred as a result of consulting this guide.

On the cover:

All cover photos are courtesy of the Dewey Whited Collection
Shapleigh Hardware Co.; St. Louis, MO, $135.00
Shumate; St. Louis, MO, $95.00
Case Brothers; Little Valley, NY, $130.00
Engels Werk, C.W. Engels; Germany, $55.00

Searching For A Publisher?

We are always looking for knowledgeable people considered to be experts within their fields. If you feel that there is a real need for a book on your collectible subject and have a large comprehensive collection, contact Collector Books.

Book design by Gina Lage
Cover design by Beth Summers

Additional copies of this book may be ordered from:

COLLECTOR BOOKS
P.O. Box 3009
Paducah, Kentucky 42002-3009

@$9.95. Add $2.00 for postage and handling.

Copyright: Roy Ritchie and Ron Stewart, 1995

DEDICATION

This book is dedicated to our wives, Bethel Ritchie and Christine Stewart, and to Shadron, Shane, and Marsha and in memory of Reginald B. Ritchie.

There are always more people involved in writing a book of this kind than appear on the cover as authors. Among those whom we owe a special note of thanks are (alphabetically):

Glenn Cartwright

Harold Deaton

Ed DeCoursey

Carl Heimerdinger

Henry Heimerdinger

Steve Koontz

Kevin Pipes

Houston Price

Mike Risner

Luther Ritchie

Lloyd Stewart

Mr. and Mrs. Dewey Whited

Rollie W. Yoder

ACKNOWLEDGMENTS

Special appreciation goes to Mr. & Mrs. Dewey Whited of Whited's Trading Post. Whited's Trading Post is located on Rt. #3, Box 401-A, Hwy 421, Bristol, TN 37620. Although they deal primarily in antiques and Indian relics, they generally carry a huge number of straight razors. Dewey says you are welcome to write (or call 615-878-4615) with your razor needs.

The contributions of Smokey Mountain Knife Works to this book have been generous. They are well known as one of the giants in cutlery collecting. Their headquarters is located near Sevierville, Tennessee. Anyone with an interest in cutlery or cutlery collecting should plan a visit. Even a person with no real interest in cutlery will be impressed with their facility — it is the world's largest cutlery store! They generally have a good stock of collectible razors. You may contact them at: Smokey Mountain Knife Works, P.O. Box 4430, Sevierville, TN 37862 or call at 1-800-251-9306.

The excellent illustrations in the overview are the result of the interpretative skills of Harold Deaton. Mr. Deaton is an artist and a teacher. He can be contacted at 209 Sycamore St., Jackson, KY 41339 (or call 606-666-7696).

This book is the authors' first attempt at producing a detailed price guide for straight razors. If it is successful, we plan to do another edition. We'd like to hear from you. If you have brands which are not listed, please send them to us along with what you consider their value. Photos are appreciated. Also if you have any questions, we'll attempt to respond, provided you have included a self-addressed stamped envelope. We will also have personalized autographed books available for the cover price plus $2.50 (U.S. funds, please) for shipping and handling. You may contact us at:

RBR Cutlery
P.O. Box 384
Hindman, KY 41822

or

R&C Books
P.O. Box 151
Combs, KY 41729

CONTENTS

PREFACE

Over sixty years of joint cutlery collecting experience has allowed us to see a lot of trends and specialties in the hobby. Since the late fifties, cutlery collecting has grown from a pastime spent on the steps of mountain courthouses to highbrow investing sometimes involving literally tens of thousands of dollars.

Recently a California auction of bowie knives, swords, and other cutlery items, saw bidders who would hold up their numbers and leave them in the air until the bidding ceased and they had made their desired purchase. The comment was heard, "Money can be replaced, but there is only one of these."

You will find few cutlery collectors who have not accumulated a few straight razors along the way. We are no exception to this. Although they have never been a dominant interest among most cutlery collectors, they have always been there.

Since the publication of our last book, *The Standard Knife Collector's Guide*, we have been contacted by a significant number of readers seeking a similar guide about straight razors. There has often been the suggestion that if one isn't in print, someone ought to write one.

A little encouragement can go a long way, especially when you were already considering the subject. We began to research the specialty of collecting straight razors and found confirmation of many of our assumptions. There are correlations which allow a system to be developed to evaluate straight razors in an organized fashion. The formula we developed is found in this book.

It is a guide for the razor collector to help him understand the ins and outs of collecting straight razors. We believe straight razor collecting to be an area of cutlery collecting that the new collector can still get in on pretty close to the ground floor. We suspect that entry in collecting "straights" now would compare with getting into pocket knife collecting in the early seventies.

It will be a long time before straight razors reach the level of investment of the bowie knives described above. (For that matter, it will be a long time before pocket knife collecting will reach that level.) However, even bowie knives began, at some time, at an interest level that compares with straight razors today.

We believe that now is a great time to begin to build a razor collection. Pick what you like and stick with it. Above all, do not lose sight of the purpose of building a collection…it's supposed to be *fun*!

Courtesy of the Dewey Whited Collection

American Products Co.
Cincinnati, OH
Handle: tortoise shell
Condition: collectible
Value: $84.00

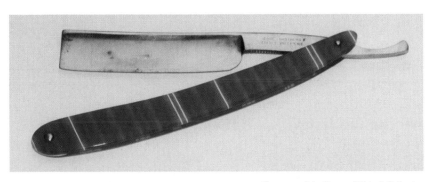

Courtesy of the Dewey Whited Collection

Case Brothers
Little Valley, NY
Handle: beautiful candy stripe celluoid
Condition: collectible
Value: $180.00

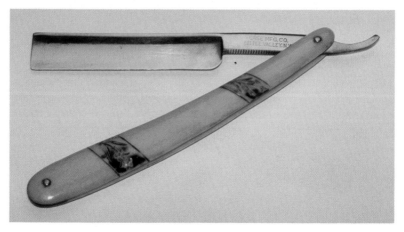

Courtesy of the Dewey Whited Collection

Case Mfg. Co.
Little Valley, NY
Handle: smooth bone, engraved and painted
Condition: collectible+
Value: $218.00

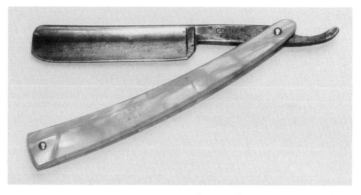

Courtesy of the Dewey Whited Collection

Case's Ace
Handle: cracked ice
Condition: collectible
Value: $75.00

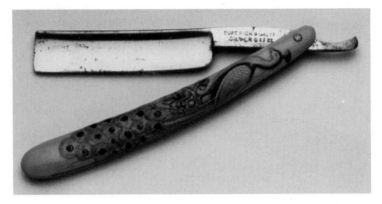

Author's Collection

Cosmo Mfg. Co.
Germany
Handle: bone, carved peacock design
Condition: good
Value: $120.00

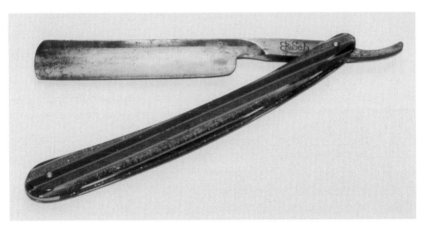

Courtesy of the Dewey Whited Collection

Ekseb
Rainbow celluloid, rare handle design
Condition: collectible
Value: $72.00

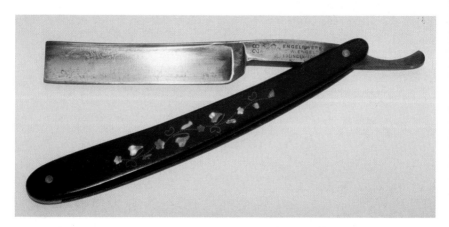

Courtesy of the Dewey Whited Collection

Engels Werk, C.W. Engels
Germany
Handle: black composition with abalone inlay and design
Condition: collectible
Value: $45.00

Courtesy of the Dewey Whited Collection

Hornet
Germany
Colorful celluloid, strap bolsters
Condition: collectible
Value: $60.00

Imperial Razor
Germany
Handle: smooth bone, Bolster & Blade etch
Condition: collectible
Value: $60.00

Jaques LeCoultre
Switzerland
Handle: black horn; brass top edge
Condition: collectible
Value: $45.00

Kinfolks
Little Valley, NY
Ivory celluloid
Condition: collectible
Value: $77.00

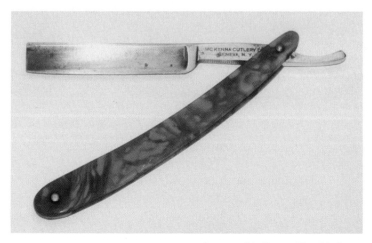

Courtesy of the Dewey Whited Collection

McKenna Cutlery
Geneva, NY
Colorful celluloid
Condition: collectible+
Value: $45.00

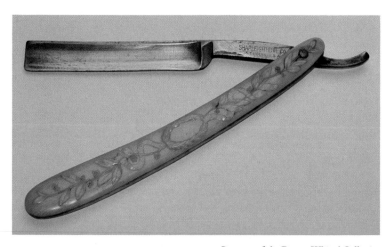

Courtesy of the Dewey Whited Collection

Shapleigh Hardware Co.
St. Louis, MO
Handle: ivory celluloid, nicely embossed
Condition: collectible
Value: $130.00

Courtesy of the Dewey Whited Collection

Shumate
St. Louis, MO
Handle: nice imitation tortoise shell
Condition: collectible
Value: $95.00

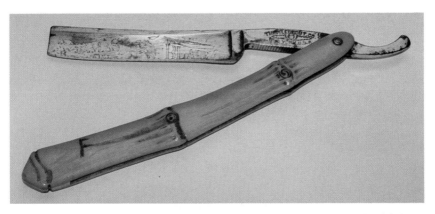

Courtesy of the Dewey Whited Collection

Thistle Cut Co.
New York, NY
Handle: genuine ivory, carved bamboo design; engraved blade
Condition: collectible
Value: $135.00

Courtesy of the Dewey Whited Collection

Union Cutlery Co.
Olean, NY
Handle: clear green plastic with imprint
Condition: collectible
Value: $35.00

Courtesy of the Dewey Whited Collection

Wade & Butcher
England
Handle: black horn, meat chopper style
Condition: collectible
Value: $144.00

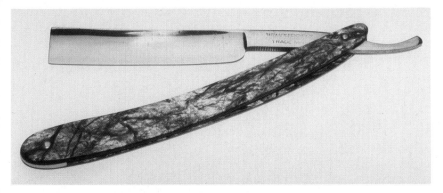

Winchester
USA
Handle: green celluloid
Condition: collectible+
Value: $170.00

Everything adds something to the value of a razor. The transition razor by Durham Duplex pictured above has the guarantee, instruction papers, and original box, adding as much as 50% to the value of the razor. It even has a coupon worth five cents! Instructions claim that it can "cut" your shaving time to two minutes! (A two minute shave with it might convince one to begin growing a beard.)

15

Boxes can add color and interest to your collection.

Pictured is Mr. Dewey Whited posing with a Tree Brand Boker display razor. The razor is one-of-a-kind. It was produced for the 1881 World's Fair/Expo. It has ivory handles which are ½" thick and gold filled blade engravings. Its value is currently estimated at between $25,000 and $35,000.

We will never know the precise stage in man's evolution when he first observed his own reflection in some still pool of clear water. We believe that, then and there, he must have decided he did not care for the dreadful appearance caused by the heavy growth of hair on his face. It may have scared the heck out of him! He probably decided, on the spot, to rid himself of the whole frightful mess. When he began to consider ways available for doing so, there were few. If he could just remove some of it, perhaps it would be a vast improvement over that hairy-faced monster he saw in the pool.

Although the old cave man's "hair mop" face did afford him some measure of protection from the elements, various creatures, and insects, it also restricted his freedom of movement. While it may have kept his mug warmer in the icy blasts of winter, it tended to hold an uncomfortable amount of heat during the hot days of summer. Even more detrimental, it was always a dangerous fire hazard when building a campfire, cooking, or warming his food. Ridding himself of the hair must not have been a difficult decision to make. The old cave man began immediately to cast about for the best method to accomplish the seemingly mundane task.

Anthropologists are inclined to inform us that in the pre-historic past, before even a trace of recorded civilization was known to exist, it was not uncommon to find tribes, even whole cultures, where the practice for removing unwanted facial hair was a common ritual among the men.

In 1991, a fully clothed and well-equipped corpse was found frozen and preserved in an Alpine glacier between Austria and Italy. It had been incarcerated for 5,300 years. The frozen corpse was relatively clean shaven! This amazing discovery pushed (shaved) the time when man began to make his first efforts at shaving, back to the beginning of the Copper Age...or perhaps beyond!

The Ice Man's beard was found to be neatly clipped to about ¼" from his facial skin. Judging from the condition and quality of his skin, clothing, and other equipment, he was in many respects a "dandy" of his time. However, he was probably just one of the many common members in his tribal society.

We do know that the removal of facial hair, as it was practiced in his time, was a far cry from the clean shaving we know today. The process was destined to evolve through the centuries as a hapless and often painful experience, learned by trial and error. Before arriving at the modern concept of bare skin shaving, there was *much* blood let.

SHAVING IN PREHISTORIC TIMES

Even before the beginning of written history, ancient man had experimented with various techniques for removing unwanted hair from his face, neck, shoulders, and forehead. Areas of particular interest were where hair could cover eyes and block one's vision. Doubtlessly, this was first done for safety reasons. However man, being the vain creature that he has always been, allowed his ego to play a role in the continuation of this act.

His first effort at removing hair, we believe, came about by sheer accident when the cave man's beard caught ablaze when he got too close to the campfire. The technique of removing hair from one's face with fire is risky, at best, to anyone...cave man or modern man. However, our old furry-faced ancestor, using small fire-brands from his campfire would torch some hair on his face and let it burn briefly, or until it became barely endurable. Then he would quickly douse it with something wet. The same process would then be repeated numerous times, until the skin became too raw or a somewhat satisfactory appearance was attained. It is doubtful that the resulting appearance was improved by any appreciable degree. However, a lot of the annoying hair had been removed. The resulting "new look" may have resembled that of an old ape, who had just survived a devastating forest fire.

We find it reasonable to assume that due to pain and hazards, this method of hair removal became largely abandoned as soon as a less torturous removal technique was found. Research indicates that this mode of "shaving" lingered in some aboriginal tribes for many centuries. Nearly concurrent with the "burn off" method of hair removal, a less hazardous (but no less painful) alternative practice began. This method consisted simply of yanking the beard out, a few hairs at a time.

Early tribes living in the equatorial zone, apparently developed beards that were much lighter than those of their northern cousins. These "Southerners" were probably the first to adopt the practice of "yanking." Having less beard to extract surely made their job easier. And...it did not grow back too fast when it had been yanked.

We doubt that anyone is using this method of facial hair removal today. However, it is used on other parts of the anatomy, such as eyebrows, eye lashes, feminine mustaches, and unwanted nasal and ear hair. Even monkeys and chimps utilize the "yanking" method of removing unwanted body hair.

It could not have been long after man became aware of himself and his appearance that he began to make use of some natural objects in his environment to help him to accomplish some of his personal tasks. For plucking out hair, he soon devised a primitive type of tweezers from tree branches that would bend together without breaking. These were used until it was found that still better results could be obtained by using clamshells, with their cartilage hinges still intact. One can easily imagine that if this method is rigidly adhered to, it could result in a totally bare and permanently hairless skin. (We'd rather not speculate about the texture of the complexion after the treatment.)

This is the method said to have been favored by most tribes of American Indians, who continued using it even after they developed excellent flint knives that were sharp enough to shave. It took on a social significance. Beyond the agony and pain, it proved the difference between a mature warrior and an adolescent boy, for those who could endure it.

Soon man's growing familiarity with a variety of cutting edge tools, such as sharp pieces of stone or shell that he fashioned into hand axes, knives, and arrowheads, were fashioned into hair cutting instruments. These beginning tools, though not advanced enough to really shave, might occasionally be sharp enough to cut off his facial hair without inflicting a serious wound. Sometimes they would cut close enough to the skin to be deemed a near shave. Often this operation, at best, would leave a ragged and very uneven beard of approximately a quarter inch in length. If the cutting edge of the stone was as sharp as they are capable of being, the operation was not a particularly painful one. With some practice it could produce an appearance close to that of a modern style beard, i.e. the "Ice Man's" beard.

During the long, dark passages of the Stone Ages there was no written history to record man's progress. However, he did manage to leave behind a few crude hieroglyphics and drawings on the walls of some caves which partly tell his story. The additional knowledge anthropologists have gleaned from countless excavations and the artifacts, such items as pottery, stone handaxes, arrow points, spears, and knives, add many enlightening facts to the story. Stone tools, during the early pre-civilized age, were refined to the point of being close to razor-sharp and were certainly capable of shaving hair.

However, this was only in some areas where a high quality, workable stone such as jasper, flint, or obsidian was readily available. Deposits of these superior type stones were formed by the terrific pressure of volcanic action that molded it into a form of natural glass. Obsidian, the hardest and best of the lot, was the most recently created material. Even today, it is sometimes used as scalpels and other surgical tools. The stones mentioned here, when broken or chipped can produce an edge similar to that of broken glass and truly as sharp.

Of course, we know that the cutting edges of Stone Age tools were always irregular and similar to the serrated edges of some modern cutlery. They could, at times, equal the cutting ability of the best grade of modern steel, but they were also brittle and easily broken. As for shaving with stone instruments, their irregular edges would have left the facial skin as maimed and bleeding as if it had been exposed to the fury of a mad bobcat.

Yet, stone knife/razors were common and have been discovered in archaeological digs in many lands. They were not, however, used for the type of shaving that we recognize today. It is not too difficult though, to envision Stone Age man grasping a wisp of his long whiskers between his forefinger and thumb while cutting it, one wisp at a time, without nicking the skin of his face.

This seems to be the type of shaving most commonly practiced in ancient times, long before the modern straight-razor made of steel came into use.

SHAVING IN THE BRONZE AGE

The Age of Copper and Bronze came and mingled with the late Stone Age over the centuries without giving vent to any outstanding or phenomenal progress in man's ceaseless search for a better way to shave and improve his appearance. A rather hefty nudge did result from an experiment in an alternate way of sharpening tools, that is, by whetting them along side their cutting edges. For this whetting or grinding, he most likely used a type of sandstone.

Man had grown accustomed to sharpening good stone tools by chipping them along their edges when they became dull and in this manner creating a sharp new edge. We also know from the "Ice

Man's" copper ax, the first metal used by man, that the cutting edge had to be hammered out. This hammering not only produced a somewhat ragged sharp cutting edge, but it greatly improved the temper and hardness of the metal. Both stone and

metal tools retained irregular cutting edges until the discovery of this new method of sharpening. Whetting had advantages which were well recognized when it came to shaving.

Since copper ranks among the softest of all metals, it did not take long, archeologically speaking, for feisty man to discover how to mix copper and a metal called zinc to produce brass or bronze. This produced an alloy which was a harder, more attractive, and more durable metal than copper. It was to serve as the major material used for cutting tools well into the Age of Iron.

The newer method of sharpening metal tools evolved into a process of whetting or grinding the sides of their cutting edges by repeatedly rubbing them against a rough stone. This likely came into practice because these early metals and metal alloys were composed of a softer substance than stone tools and could be sharpened more easily this way. While the new type cutting edge was in no way a sharper edge than chipped stone or serrated edge, it was definitely smoother and more uniform. The advantage to shaving lay in that the uniform edge cut smoothly without causing the saw-like abrasive scars left by the former. This became apparent as soon as man began using a smoother cutting edge against his face. Also, it was soon discovered that the smoother the cutting edge of the instrument, the closer one could shave or cut near the skin without scratching, nicking, or grooving the skin. If you should have any doubts about this, just try shaving sometime with an old straight razor that has just a few minute gaps along the edge!

Bronze razors, with smooth ground edges, have been discovered in the burial mounds of many ancient races. They can be found in the tombs of some Egyptian kings and queens. Although the bronze straight-edged razors constituted a vast improvement toward the close shaving instrument mankind was searching for, there was still the need for a harder and more durable edge-holding material than the bronze alloy that was then available.

So the search continued. As the Bronze Age eventually faded away into the New Age of Iron and other metal alloys, these new metals were fashioned into razors.

THE AGE OF IRON AND METAL ALLOYS

Our crystal ball tells us that it was a time before 1000 B.C., in the Near East or Western Asia depending on your research source, that a tribe of herdsmen built a very hot fire in the confined area of a roasting pit. The fire just happened to contain some stray meteorites or other stones that were rich in iron ore. For some reason, perhaps due to a hefty residue of unburned charcoal left in the ashes, the fire generated enough heat to melt the ore and leave a glowing puddle of raw iron in the ashes. When the ore cooled, its unnatural weight and intense hardness became immediately apparent. From there on, man's natural curiosity took over. His tinkering with the ore resulted in the initial discovery of iron, a metal superior to bronze. It was a metal more suitable for use in making cutting tools, weapons, and shaving devices.

Travel and commerce spread the knowledge of iron smelting and forging. The process became known far and wide. It was adapted eagerly by the more advanced cultures, especially Egypt which was recognized at the time as the most advanced civilization in the world.

Historical records, gleaned from hieroglyphics and drawings on the walls of ancient caves and pyramids, depict the first iron razors as crude affairs with large cumbersome blades. From their appearance it is not hard to visualize the similarity between shaving with them and that of our mythical Paul Bunyan shaving with this immense broad ax.

Of course, the first razors made of iron (and bronze) were not folding instruments. In reality, they were more similar to the modern day cook's meat chopper than any razor style today. Some have been discovered to have handle material fashioned from bone or wood in more refined pieces. After centuries of use and experience, the realization must have dawned that the smaller the razor's size, the easier it is to shave with it. So, with time, the massive blades grew smaller and in most cases sharper and more refined.

Yet, the old meat chopper blade did carry over into the folding area and to some degree, still prevails.

The extreme sharpness of these old blades certainly made them dangerous to transport or move about. Because of this, as soon as the

23

knowledge became available, all of the more advanced nations were quick to adapt the Roman style of sheathing their knife blades for the safety it provided.

THE "BEGINNING-STRAIGHT" STRAIGHT RAZORS

The greater part of our present population has never been aware of any type of razor except the common variety of so-called straight razors. It may be difficult for them to now perceive that the straight razor did in fact originate as a simple, straight-frame instrument that folded like a pocketknife, but never acquired a backspring. It was really very similar to the Old English "Penny Knife" that was so common during the seventeenth and eighteenth centuries. It is likely that it acquired the name "straight razor" from this period in its development. It seems this really "straight" razor served the purpose for which it was intended very well indeed! It served man through many centuries as they emerged from the Dark Ages and well after the birth of Christ. It became the shaving instrument of choice, used for the longest period of time, without any major changes.

Meanwhile, we should not overlook another important event that added greatly to the progress of shaving. This, of course, was the discovery and use of plain old soap. It doesn't take much imagination for us to visualize the stinky, messy situation we would be in today without its consistent and habitual everyday use. It became the ultimate aid for shaving!

Ancient records indicate that soap of a crude form was first discovered by the Babylonians sometime during the fading centuries of the Bronze Age. Once again we consult our crystal ball to find it is very likely that some individual, while cooking or roasting meat around a campfire, noticed the gooey stuff oozing from the ashes. This mixture consisting of animal fat and the lye in the wood ashes, when combined, formed the basic ingredients of raw soap. So we assume that when the fellow who was fondly roasting the nice fat pig for his dinner, accidentally got the sticky stuff on his hands, face, and maybe hair and then attempted to wash it off, he found it also washed off all of the remaining dirt and grease from his skin. Theoretically then, soap was discovered. Yet, the time closed in on "zero" B.C. before it became widely accepted and habitually used by the more nearly civilized nations.

Soap then, was finally recognized as a tremendous aid in the shaving process. With that soapy lather to soften the beard on his face and cause the blade to glide smoothly over the surface of his skin, mankind was at long last nearing the final step to a smooth, clean, and comfortable shave.

Today, it is hard to imagine shaving off a day's growth of beard without the ameliorating effect of soap or shaving cream. If encountered today, it would be called a dry-shave. Even though it might help a little to soak the beard in plain water, it would still be a desperate and painful experience.

When I think about this, I am always reminded of the joke my father used to tell his customers. It was about a simple country boy who had worked himself out a nice little jag of money and decided to take it into town to celebrate his good fortune. In the small country town the first thing that caught his eye was the bright red and white striped barber pole of the town's barber shop. So he decided to get himself a store-bought shave...for the first time in his life.

All he could think of about this kind of shaving was remembering knife traders talk about the advantage of dry shaving, which was in

reality a method they used of shaving hair off their arms to test the sharpness of their knives. But from this, the young man concluded that dry shaving must be the very best kind.

So, he informed the jovial barber that he wanted none other than a dry shave. The barber questioned his decision, but the boy persisted and the process began.

From the very beginning he was twisting and squirming from the burning, excruciating pain but doing his darndest to be a man and not cry out.

Then, just about the time he had reached the breaking point, an old jenny mule that some farmer had left hitched nearby, gave vent to a thunderous braying that literally shook the whole town, causing everyone to rear up and ask, "Now what-the-hell was that?"

The boy in the barber chair reared up too, with a smart grin on his raw and ruddy face, said "I know what it was! It was some other damn fool getting a dry-shave!"

For us, this seems to illustrate the great advantage soap and shaving creams contribute to the process of shaving.

THE "NON-STRAIGHT" STRAIGHT RAZOR

When we pursue the evolution of shaving instruments, we find that the original, old straight-frame folding razor was in use for multiple centuries before it finally began the transformation which gave it the familiar look it presents today. We also find that there were good and practical reasons for the seemingly strange and unusual alterations.

When we pick up one of these later instruments and hold it in the usual mode for use, we will realize quickly that these features were not intended as innovations to make it more attractive. They were actually designed to make holding the razor steadier and at the proper angle for doing a good, safe job of shaving.

Since the razor is always held for use about one fourth less than fully open, we notice that the thumb and index finger pinch the inner tang, while the middle finger loops over the outer tang or "monkey tail." The two remaining fingers fold around the frame to hold it firmly in place. With this grip, the entire instrument is held steady and it is easy to change the angle of the cut while shaving.

These, and other modifications that greatly improved the efficiency of the modern straight razor, seemed to have been developed mostly during the late eighteenth and early nineteenth centuries after barbering and barber shops had become popular and well-established social institutions.

Of course, any man possessing a steady hand could shave himself at home. But, visiting the barber shop was thought of as a luxury and gave an individual the appearance of being of some esteem on the social scale. By doing this at least once a week for a shave and once a month for a haircut, he kept a neat appearance and avoided lots of little nicks and scratches.

The local barber shop was also a sort of men's club, where the barber always kept the best and sharpest types of shaving instruments. He was always ready to dispense with the latest news along with a soothing shave and a refreshing after-shave tonic. The men usually returned home feeling so up-beat and smelling so good that their wives were glad to have them go. In addition, the value of the good gossip he picked up could not be underestimated.

So in all likelihood, it was these barbers of the 1800s and 1900s who called the shots for bringing about most of the major improvements in the straight razors. We know that the tempering of steel and

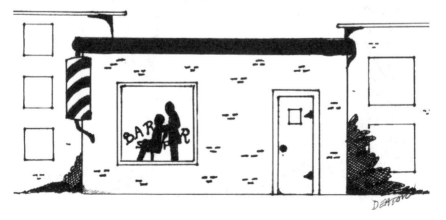

steel alloys were developed to a high degree of perfection. Also, the long standing system of grinding the blades at a slant from the spline (their back edge) down to the cutting edge was developed. This was known as the wedge grind. It was mostly abandoned during the seventeenth century for the more productive concave shape hollow grind.

The hollow grind blade is thinner along the cutting edge and thicker along the spline. Because of this, the blade cuts better, stays sharper longer, and is easier to sharpen when it does become dull. The hollow grind blade was in fact, a vast improvement over the wedge grind. It was doubtlessly the last major improvement for the straight razors (before their decline).

Research indicates that straight razors, which are also known as cut-throat razors, reached the peak of their popularity during the late 1800s and early 1900s. During this time they were regarded as essential items for every household in the civilized world. Their decline was hastened by the introduction of the safety razor.

The replacement's name provides a major clue to the rapid shift away from the straight razor. The old cut-throat straight razor was simply a sometimes lethal, and often a safety, liability in the home. Due to its intrinsic qualities it constituted a distinct peril to amateur users, those with shaky hands, and of course, children (who found them an irresistible toy with which to harm themselves).

When we consider all this, it is not difficult to foresee the final phasing out of the old straight razor's lengthy and dominant niche in the American home.

At the beginning of the eighteenth century every major cutlery company in America manufactured an abundance of straight razors for the domestic trade. By mid-century they had mostly ceased production in their own factories. Since it was less cost consuming to supply the greatly diminished demand, they quickly diverted to selling imported razors from European countries such as England and Germany.

RAZOR COLLECTING

It was in the early 1960s, about the same time that pocketknife collecting began to be recognized as one of the fastest growing hobbies in the collecting field, that a modest number of knife collectors began taking a second look at straight razors. The finer, more ornate ones caught their attention. At the time, literally bushels of the old razors could be found strewn about in every nook and cranny that one chose to look. They were cheap, often in the way, and something with which the children could get cut. They were sold for almost anything. Nickels and dimes were not unheard of prices for many of them.

As rare and antique knives began becoming scarce and their prices began to soar, many collectors began looking for a new collectible that they could get into on the ground floor. The abundance of straight razors became more noticeable...and certainly more interesting.

The similar characteristics of the razors to knives did not go unnoticed by knife collectors. These had an advantage in that they could be added to existing cutlery collections and serve to make the collection more interesting. They could also be picked up at comparably very reasonable prices. Knife collectors with vision became interested and took the steps that led to their investing in them.

It was to be some time, however, before they were considered as little more than a sideline to knives and other related collectibles in the field of cutlery. You could see them turning up at flea markets more and more frequently. At the really big gun and knife shows, someone almost always had a few. Often they were placed around the fringes to add variety, color, and some interest to large cutlery displays. Displays at knife shows share a common characteristic with viruses. They're catching. The urge to invest in the more attractive of the available razors was just too strong for many collectors to resist.

It was only a matter of time before straight razors began to gain in popularity. In the 1970s and 1980s their popularity continued to increase. Finds were still around. Bargains could still be found with some frequency if a person was willing to look hard. They were considered to be good long-term investments.

Now, in the 1990s, straight razors are more popular than ever, with the peak of the ole whisker-getters nowhere in sight. Surely, this is understandable. After all, many of these old razors were handled with very precious materials. Often, they were embellished with some of the finest artwork of their time.

Even though, at this time, there are only a handful of collectors who collect straight razors exclusively, it would be a mistake to overlook the investment potential of this class of cutlery. Indeed, this arena still has lots of room for the investor who wants to move in on a lower floor. The future is bright! There are lots of private households and vintage residential sections that have not yet been exposed to razor collecting. Estate auctions often sell razors by the cigar box full! They can still (sometimes) be found for very inexpensive prices in flea markets where activity in razor collecting has not hit.

Of course, many new collectors have missed a lot of fabulous finds, but they can still discover hidden treasures in often the most unexpected places. However, you should not expect to find very many real sleepers or big bargains around knife and gun shows anymore.

During the heydays of straight razor use, from the mid 1800s through the early 1900s, almost every household possessed from one single usable razor to a deluxe seven piece weekly set. These were kept ready and available for the personal and private use of the owner. Whether lord of the manor or common field hand, men cherished their personal razors so highly that they seemed to become an extension of their ego and pride.

Because of this, most cutlery firms used the finest and most expensive materials, including gold and silver, in their construction. They decorated these fine razors with artwork of the most superb craftsmen/artists available. These most magnificent razors were usually owned by the more affluent. The decorative razor was not cheap to produce, but the manufacturer could still charge a price which would more than pay for the aesthetic ornamentation.

As odd as it may appear, straight razors never really evolved beyond the one basic pattern. All their different designs ran along similar lines. In sizes though, they ranged all the way from the gigantic meat chopper to the dainty little corn or lady shavers. The medium sized cut throat razor was the most preferred and thus, the most common size produced by manufacturers. Over the years, this razor became the standard.

The common pattern range, is compensated for by the wide range of rare, luxurious handle materials and designs that were used on straight razors of all sizes. Metals were not uncommon handle materials. Choices for complete scales included brass, aluminum, and silver. Gold and platinum were generally reserved for ornamental trim work such as bolsters, escutchions, and inlay. When complete handles were made of metal, they were almost always decorated with pleasing, pressed or carved designs.

In the early stages of straight razor development, all metals (including aluminum) were considered to be expensive. This was all the more reason for metal to be selected for razor handle materials. After all, nothing was considered too good for those elegant old straight razors!

The same criteria also applied to the other fine, natural and manmade materials which were used for handles. In order of their collector value, tortoise shell and elephant ivory top the list. It should be noted that the use of both materials was not prohibited by law to protect the species. They are not legally available today. However, they were used routinely in the manufacture of old straight razors, during the 1800s and early part of this century.

Genuine pearl and Indian stag were other natural materials which were available on demand. They were plentiful at the time.

Because of their perishable nature, the old celluloids are becoming so scarce they may soon be extinct. This versatile old material with its ability to hold colors in brilliant, lucid shades and a wide range of transparent forms, was truly remarkable. The ease of molding celluloid and shaping it into products of outstanding beauty, appeared to be almost magical. There was "gold and silver sparkle," "candy stripe," "Christmas tree," "waterfall," and countless other designs in all the colors of the rainbow. Of course these were in the old vintage celluloid that modern plastics can never expect to equal.

Then horn and bone in natural, color dyed, and worked variety, are other natural materials that have remained in more available supply and common use. The picked or dyed bone is rare on old razors, but slick white is rather common. As for horn, the lighter more transparent variety was once a much sought after novelty, but for their beauty collectors are seeking the stained, molded, and sometimes carved horn scales that are really outstanding for their artwork.

Plain black horn is the most common color, and likewise of the least collector value unless it is artworked in some medium. Following up are the other synthetics and man-made fibrous groups such as old hard rubber and Bakelite materials that, while not so colorful, were still easy to mold and shape into pleasing, useful designs. Although they were usually breakable and of one color, they are special collectibles if artworked and without flaws.

Most of these older, man-made synthetics have given way to modern plastics and resins. While modern plastic simulations cannot match the glowing beauty of the older synthetics, they are more durable and less expensive to manufacture.

So when our country's infinite crop of straight razors finally did pass the peak of their constant domestic use, they began losing ground to the more recent safety shaving devices of various designs. Then a plain black handle material of cheap modern plastic became the common and most standard material for all razor scales.

FACTORS THAT DETERMINE COLLECTOR VALUE

When we consider the things that determine collector value, we find there are an enormous number of factors that could have an effect. However, the major factors to consider are the ones previously discussed and their varying degrees of influence on collector value. With this in mind, we have devised a simple formula, that is easy to manipulate, for finding the collector value of collectible razors.

The razor's brand name and country of origin are major items in determining value, as well as being the source of identification. American-made brands rank higher in value to the American collector than most imports. Those manufactured by outstanding gun or cutlery firms (such as Remington or Case) are at the very top of the list. One reason for this is that straight razors have ceased to be manufactured in the United States. Although there were hundreds (thousands) of American manufacturers, this country was never the world's top producer of straight razors. So if it was made in the U.S., it is often an older item than the quantities of razors that were made in England or Germany. Subsequently these razors are generally rarer and reasonably collectible.

During the 1800s, England and Germany consistently supplied the U.S. with the bulk of its straight razors. Later, German-made ones were the most common. Both countries were host to some great old firms and produced razors that rank very high in collector value. Other countries, too, produced some impressive razors. To be thorough in your collecting effort, don't overlook the ones made in foreign countries. The razors produced in many of these countries have a surprisingly high value to some collectors.

Even though there are those who will loudly disagree with us, we believe that only brief notice should be paid to the different styles and sizes of straight razors. Size, shape, blade design, all evolved within the same basic straight razor pattern. Generally, the differences do not appear to play a major role in the collector value of the straight razor.

Of course, there are exceptions to this rule. A notable one is that of the old great meat-chopper model. This razor, arguably, bears more resemblance to a meat cleaver than to a straight razor. (Perhaps this tells us something of its effectiveness!) Collectors who seek only this style of straight razor, will indeed pay a premium. This may be up to three or four times that of a normal straight razor by the same manufacturer.

As straight razor collecting evolves, we predict that even more specialties will surface. Collectors who are interested in purchasing/collecting razors with particular characteristics, will invariably cause those characteristics to impact the overall value of razors.

However, handle material and the artwork and design of the handles are other matters entirely! The genuine natural materials that were used for handles add significantly to the razor's value. The more rare the material today, the higher the collector value of the razor. Materials common at the time of manufacture often have become uncommon since. Ivory, for example, has become about as scarce as hen's teeth or frog hair. However, during the heyday of the straight razor, the use of ivory was not unusual at all. When it comes to value, the relatively modern straight razor with plastic handles has little in common with the razor that has scales of the scarcer natural materials from the past. The type of materials used to handle the old straight razor undoubtedly plays a significant role in establishing today's collector value of the piece.

The more prized and expensive razors of yesteryear had handles which were ornately designed. These designs were produced by some of the most highly skilled artisans of their day. This was when computer design and computer etching were undreamed of! The handle designs and etchings were often done one at a time and thus became one-of-a-kind razors because of the elaborate work of the artist.

The art to which we refer includes any carving, scrimshaw, painting, or design on the handles. Scrollwork or designs on the blade and rattail should also be included in this category. Ornate bolsters or tip pieces, inlays, and even advertising, all add to the artistic value of the ole face scrapers.

Since artwork is an added decor, it can be graded separately and in addition to the value of handle materials. The type of the artwork and the skill of the artist are factors in determining the value added by the artwork. Your best and most critical judgment must be utilized in noting the type and quality of this work. The skill of the artist inevitably adds to or subtracts from the value of the enhanced razor.

Remember, these pieces were an owner's source of pride. They were expensive in their day. They were considered special and were treated as such. Today's collector should recognize that these ornate razors are accustomed to special treatment and should continue the practice.

The experienced appraiser of the artwork found on ornate razors, would feel right at home in the company of one who evaluates scrimshaw or cameos. It could literally take years to gain the experience and do the research required to be recognized as an authority.

However, such skills are not absolutely required by the collector. They can tell you what they like, why it appeals to them, and generally just what they are wiling to pay for a piece that fits their desires. Part of the fun of collecting is to collect what you like. Judging from their collections, a lot of collectors seem to be doing pretty well for themselves.

The value of experience should never be underestimated! A beginning collector should always be willing to seek the advice of the experienced collector before jumping in with both feet.

Some of the more common types of decorative artwork are listed below. We consider these to be somewhat in the order of the value that collectors assign to them. They are:

Sculpture
Carving
Gold Inlay
Embossed or Pressed Design
Scrimshaw
Picture Window
Silver Inlay
Pearl or Abalone Inlay
Bronze Inlay
Bolsters
Pin Studding
Deco Designs
Script
Colorful
Advertising Art
Logo Art

We believe that this area needs a bit more fine-tuning, so the ranking will be adjusted into the following categories: Superior, Very Good, Average, Minimal, and Plain.

Next, the *condition* of the razor will be considered as the last factor used in the appraisal chart. Since by this time we are near to being certain that straight razors will never be used again in our homes for private shaving, we will not even consider relegating them to such chaste ratings as mint or excellent. Having observed how little consideration collectors show for condition, unless it is damaged beyond repair, we have decided that a minimum amount of rating and fine-tuning is all that is necessary.

For maximum ease in the operation of the appraisal formula, we have all condition stages falling directly into three broad categories: the Good, the Collectibles, and the Parts Razor.

The Good will contain no conspicuous or highly visible flaws. Especially none that cannot be erased by an expert repair job.

The Collectibles can show a small amount of rust, pitting, stain, fading, chipping, cracking, and wear, as long as it does not seriously detract from the instrument's overall appearance after restoration and display.

The Parts Razors are generally considered as razors that are damaged beyond repair. Yet, even the Parts Razors have some value. They usually contain parts that can be salvaged and used in other razors for repair. They sometimes contain the parts needed to complete a damaged razor and turn it into a beautiful instrument.

In our opinion, the factors having the most influence and importance on determining the value of a straight razor are:

Brand Name and Origin
Handle Material
Artwork
Condition

By utilizing these four areas, we have constructed the following charts and devised the following formula for finding an old straight razor's comparative collector value. We sincerely believe that this deduced collector value will be a workable one that will protect the collector from paying too much or selling too cheaply. It was devised after years of market experience and gathering and checking statistics. We believe it will be as close, if not closer, to a true collector value than any other razor scale available. At the very least, if utilized properly, it should serve to keep you out of trouble.

APPRAISAL CHART

To find the collector value of your razor, multiply (a) times (b), then multiply (a) times (c), add the two answers and multiply this sum times (d). The answer you get is (e), your collector value.

(a)	(b)
Brand and Origin Base Value	Handle Material % Value
Look up your razor in the Listings of Companies & Base Values and note the base value.	*Find your handle material, determine its percentage value (b), and multiply it by the base value (a). After multiplying, convert your percentage answer to a dollar value.*

Handle Material	% value
Ivory	550%
Tortoise Shell	500%
Silver	500%
Abalone	450%
Pearl	400%
Stag	400%
Bone	
Picked	350%
Jigged	350%
Smooth	300%
Aluminum	350%
Celluloid	
Colorful	300%
Solid Color	275%
Picture/Advertising	250%
Cracked Ice	250%
Horn	
Clear	275%
Dyed	250%
Black	200%
"Slick Black"	150%
Composition	150%
Bakelite	150%
Hard Rubber	150%
Wood	150%
Modern Plastics	100%
Fiber	75%

$$(a) \times (b) = A$$
$$(a) \times (c) = B$$
$$A + B = C$$
$$C \times (d) = (e)$$

(c)	(d)	(e)
Artwork % Value	Condition % Value	Collector Value
Select the percentage that best describes your razor's art (c) and multiply it by the base value (a). Convert your percentage answer to a dollar value.	*Select the percentage that is nearest to your razor (d). (You may rate your razor between the described percentages, i.e. 125%.)*	*To determine the Collector Value of your razor, now add the dollar amounts you found in (b) and (c) together.*
		Multiply that sum times the condition value you determined in (d).
Superior 550% Good 400% Average 300% Minimal 200% Plain 100% Nonexistent 0%	Good 150% Collectible 100% Parts 10%	
The evaluation of artwork is very subjective. The usual types of artwork found on razors are listed below in ascending values. The quality of the artwork as well as the type, plays a role in determining its value.	Good has no visible or outstanding flaws that cannot be erased or repaired.	*This gives you the Collector Value of your razor (e).*
Sculpture Carving Gold Inlay Embossed or Pressed Design Scrimshaw Picture Window Silver Inlay Pearl or Abalone Inlay Bronze Inlay Bolsters Pin Studding Deco Designs Script Colorful Advertising Art Logo Art	Collectible has some flaws that do greatly detract from the artwork or finish. Parts are unrepairable and have value only for salvageable parts.	

APPRAISING YOUR RAZOR

A walk through, utilizing our appraisal chart and our listing of razor companies, should be instructive in properly determining the value of your razor. Let us look at each category:

•Brand Name and Origin Base Value: This is the value for a plain razor, with plastic handles, no artwork, in collectible condition. This is the value to which enhancements in handle material, artwork, and condition will be added or subtracted. To determine this value for your razor, just look up the name of the razor in our chart listing of companies.

•Handle Material Value: This value is determined by multiplying the base value of your razor, by the handle material percentage found on the appraisal chart. Convert this to a dollar value.

•Artwork Value: This value is a bit subjective, but by studying the artwork listing, from most valued types of artwork to the least, you can determine if the artwork on your razor is superior, good, average, minimal, plain, or nonexistent.

To obtain the value of this category, simply multiply the Base Value times the Artwork percentage which you have determined fits your razor's artwork. Convert this to a dollar value.

•Condition Value: This is the most subjective category of evaluation. You must determine the condition of the razor and where it falls between barely parts (junk?) 10% and good (great?) 150%. We use the term collectible to describe the middle range of 100%. You are not stuck with the three percentage categories. For example, you may determine that your razor may be collectible+ at 125% or collectible- at 80%. A parts+ razor might be rated at 48% or an obviously superior piece could go off the chart at good+ 175%.

Look your razor over closely. Review the categories described by the chart and determine the razor's percentage condition. (Be honest.) When you have done this, you are ready to determine the Collector Value of your razor.

•Collector Value: Simply take the Handle Material Value and add it to the Artwork Value. Then take the sum of these two values and multiply it times the Condition percentage. When you convert the percentage figure to a dollar amount by marking off two places and putting a decimal point in place, you have the Collector Value of your razor.

If your figure seems out of line, check your math. If there are no mistakes in your math, check on your appraisal in each category, make revisions, and repeat the process.

Now, let's walk through this with the following example (calculated examples are scattered throughout the book):

Step 1: Brand and Origin. Simmons Hardware Co., St. Louis, MO (look up the company in our Listings of Companies and Base Values). The base value is $18.00.

Courtesy of Smokey Mountain Knife Works

(a) Brand and Origin Base Value	(b) Handle Material % Value	(c) Artwork % Value	(d) Condition % Value	(e) Collector Value
Simmons Hardware Co. St. Louis, MO **$18.00**	Ivory Celluloid 18 x 300%= **$54.00**	Standing nude w/ rose 18 x 350%= **$63.00**	Collectible- **90%**	$54 + $63= $117 $117 x 90%= $105.30 **$105.00**

Step 2: Handle Material. The handle material of this razor is Ivory Celluloid. The percentage investment value for celluloid is 300%.

Multiply your base value ($18.00) times your Handle Material Value (300%) and you have a figure of $54.00.

Step 3: Artwork. An embossed standing nude surrounded by roses graces the handles. We determine the artwork percentage enhancement to be above average, at about 350%. We then multiply the base value ($18.00) times the artwork enhancement percentage (350%) or $18.00 x 350%= $63.00.

Step 4: Condition. A close examination reveals some stains and discoloration on the handles and a small pin crack. We determine the condition to be around 90%.

Step 5: Collector Value. To determine the Collector Value, add the Handle Material Value ($54.00) to the Artwork Value ($63.00) = ($117.00). Then multiply this total ($117.00) by the condition percentage (90%). This equals $105.30. Forget the 30 cents. The Collector Value of the razor is $105.00.

Simply put Base Value x Handle Material Value ($54.00) + Base Value x Artwork Value ($63.00) = $117.00. The sum of these values ($117.00) x the Condition Value (90%) = Collector Value ($105.00).

Since parts of this system are subjective, the determination of the value of some aspects of the razor depends on the collector. Different values may be arrived at by different collectors for the same razor. If the values of each category agree, however, there should be no reason the final calculation should not agree. The determination of the subjective values leaves room for negotiations and dickering. It would not be nearly as much fun if everything was cut and dried. That kind of objectivity can be found at Wal-Mart. So, be cautioned, these values are not set in stone. They should not be. The taste of collectors varies from person to person as to the way they value different parts of a razor. For example, while one person may find artwork of a nude to be beautiful another may be offended by it. The subjective evaluation of the razor may differ between the two collectors.

If you use our evaluation system with care, you will find that it works well as a guide. It should provide you with a reliable comparison collector value of the razors you inspect.

And remember our advice...collecting is supposed to be *fun!*

* **Indicates photo and chart are shown**

LISTINGS OF COMPANIES & BASE VALUES

COMPANY	BASE VALUE
A 1, A. Witte; England	$10.00
AAA 1, A.J. Jordan; England	$10.00
Abarams, G.D. & Sons; Wayland, NY	$10.00
Abdoo, T.; Germany	$9.00
Abercrombie & Finch; NY	$11.00
Abound & Boosamara; Germany	$9.00
A.B.T. Co. (Aerial); USA	$20.00
Adair Barber Supply; England/USA	$10.00
Adair, Charles W. & Co.; Danville, IL	$9.00
Adams; Germany	$10.00
Adams, Charles; USA/Germany	$10.00
Adams & Sons; USA/Germany	$10.00
Adell Mfg. Co.; England	$10.00
Adelsdorfer Bros.; Germany	$9.00
Adelsdorfer, John C.; Germany	$9.00
* Admiral; England/Germany/RI	$12.00

Courtesy of Smokey Mountain Knife Works

(a) Brand and Origin Base Value	(b) Handle Material % Value	(c) Artwork % Value	(d) Condition % Value	(e) Collector Value
The Admirals, Germany using Sheffield Steel **$12.00**	Candystripe Celluloid 12 x 300%= **$36.00**	Etchings of Admirals Dewey, Schleg & Sampson, molded handles 12 x 300%= **$36.00**	Collectible **100%**	$36 + $36=$72 $72 x 100%= **$72.00**

Adolphus Cutlery; Germany	$11.00
* Aerial Cutlery Co.; WI	$22.00

Courtesy of Smokey Mountain Knife Works

(a) Brand and Origin Base Value	(b) Handle Material % Value	(c) Artwork % Value	(d) Condition % Value	(e) Collector Value
Aerial Cutlery Mfg. Co. Marinette, WI **$22.00**	Clear Celluloid 22 x 300%= **$66.00**	Pictures of four ladies, 20's style 22 x 200%= **$44.00**	Collectible **100%**	$66 + $44= $110 $110 x 100%= **$110.00**

Aesculap	$10.00
Aeuos; Germany	$9.00
Aevas Razor Co.	$10.00
Agard Hardware Co.; Torrington, CT	$10.00
A.H.A. Co.; WA	$10.00
A.I.C. (Allegheny Instrument Co.); Allegheny, NY	$11.00
Akers-Britton & Co.; IN	$11.00
Akron, K. & J. Co.; Akron, OH	$9.00
Albert & Meyer; Germany	$10.00
Albert, Schmidt, Nachf; Germany	$16.00
* Albrecht, F.W., Barber Supply House; Akron, OH	$12.00

Courtesy of Smokey Mountain Knife Works

(a) Brand and Origin Base Value	(b) Handle Material % Value	(c) Artwork % Value	(d) Condition % Value	(e) Collector Value
F.W. Albrecht's B.S. House; Akron, OH Blue Steel, Germany **$12.00**	Sterling Silver 12 x 500%= **$60.00**	High relief floral design 12 x 400%= **$48.00**	Good **150%**	$60 + $48= $108 $108 x 150%= **$162.00**

Alcapisi, J.P.; Schenectady, NY	$10.00
Alcoso Stahlwarenfabrik; Germany	$10.00
Allegheny Instrument Co.; Allegheny, NY	$11.00
Allen, Joseph & Sons; England	$10.00
Alliance Cutlery Works; Philadelphia, PA	$15.00
Allison; USA/Germany	$10.00
Alloway & Sons; Salem, MA	$10.00
Alpha Razor Co.; Chicago, IL	$11.00
Altenbach & Sons; Germany	$10.00
Althoff, Henry; Geneva, NY	$10.00
Alwin; Germany	$10.00
Amco-Royal Crown Instrument Corp.; Germany	$10.00
American Barber Tool; Philadelphia, PA	$10.00
American Cutlery Co.; St. Louis, MO	$10.00
American Cutlery Co.; Chicago, IL	$10.00
American Knife Co.; Plymouth Hollow, CT	$10.00
American Knife Co.; Newark, NJ	$15.00
American Products Co.; Cincinnati, OH	$12.00
American Stock Food Co.; Fremont, OH	$8.00
Anchor Razor	$8.00
Angyan, B.; Budapest, Hungary	$9.00
Antoberg, Erik; Sweden	$11.00
Antonitadross; Germany	$10.00
Appleton & Lichfield; Boston, MA	$15.00
* Aranatelli, V.; Palermo, Italy	$12.00

Courtesy of Smokey Mountain Knife Works

(a) Brand and Origin Base Value	(b) Handle Material % Value	(c) Artwork % Value	(d) Condition % Value	(e) Collector Value
V. Aranatelli Palermo, Italy **$12.00**	Black Composition 12 x 150%= **$18.00**	Picture handle 12 x 350%= **$42.00**	Good **150%**	$18 + $42=$60 $60 x 150%= **$90.00**

Arbenz, Ad; France	$10.00
3 B Co.; Akron, OH	$9.00
Bailey's Choice, Martin & Gannaway; Lynchburg, VA	$10.00
Baker & Co.; England	$12.00
Baker & Co. Inc., Edward J. Hornell; NY	$12.00
* Baker, C.; Solingen, Germany	$10.00

Courtesy of Smokey Mountain Knife Works

(a) Brand and Origin Base Value	(b) Handle Material % Value	(c) Artwork % Value	(d) Condition % Value	(e) Collector Value
C. Baker; Solingen, Germany **$10.00**	Ivory Celluloid 10 x 300%= **$30.00**	Stand nude w/ morning glory 10 x 450%= **$45.00**	Good **150%**	$30 + $45=$75 $75 x 150%= $112.50 **$113.00**

Bakers, J & T; England	$10.00
Bakersfield Barber Supply Co.; Bakersfield, CA	$18.00
Balding & Co; NY	$8.00
Baldwin, Robbins; Boston, MA	$10.00
Balk, Wilson	$7.00
Baltuch	$10.00
Baltzay Co.; Massillon, OH	$10.00

Bammer, August; Germany	$9.00
Bammer, August & Son; Germany	$9.00
Banard	$9.00
Bankowski	$8.00
* Bannister, A.J. & Co.; Newark, NJ	$10.00

Courtesy of Smokey Mountain Knife Works

(a) Brand and Origin Base Value	(b) Handle Material % Value	(c) Artwork % Value	(d) Condition % Value	(e) Collector Value
A.J. Bannister & Co. Newark, NJ **$10.00**	Yellow & Red Celluloid 10 x 300%= **$30.00**	Notched blade 10 x 110%= **$11.00**	Collectible **100%**	$30 + $11=$41 $41 x 100%= **$41.00**

Bannister & Clark; Newark, NJ	$10.00
Barber	$9.00
Barber, I.; England	$9.00
Barber, John; England	$10.00
Barber Supply Co.; Lincoln, NE	$12.00
Barber's Delight; USA	$10.00
Barber's Gem	$9.00
Barhep; Germany	$9.00
Barlow, Adam; England	$12.00
Barlow, James & Son; England	$11.00
Barnes, Edward & Sons; England	$11.00
Barnes, Fredrick; England	$10.00
Barnes, Josia; England	$11.00
Barnsley Brothers Cutlery Co.; Monett, MO	$15.00
Barry, James G.; Chicago, IL	$15.00
Bartmann; Germany	$8.00
Bates, C.J. & Sons; Chester, CT	$15.00
Battle Ax Cutlery; Philadelphia, PA	$18.00
Bauer Mfg. & Co.; San Francisco, CA	$12.00

Baughman, W.H. Co.; Akron, OH	$10.00
Baumann Barber Supply Co.; Cincinnati, OH	$10.00
Baumgartner Hardware Co.	$9.00
Baurmann, Friedt & Sohne; Germany	$10.00
Bavar Beauty & Barber Supply Co.	$9.00
Baxter; USA	$8.00
Bayside Cutlery; WI	$18.00
Bay State Manufacturing Co.; MA	$22.00
B & B Supply Co.; Dayton, OH	$10.00
Beau-Brummel Cutlery; Germany	$12.00
Beaudette; Holyoke, MA	$10.00
Beauty Supply Co.; Canton, OH	$10.00
Becker, Gebr.; Germany	$8.00
Belk, G.W.; England (?)	$8.00
Belknap Hardware & Manufacturing Co.; Louisville, KY	$18.00
Bell Barber Supply Co.; Germany	$8.00
Bell, Gebr.; Germany	$8.00
Belle Fountaine, Ltd.; England	$12.00
Belmount Mfg. Co.; USA	$10.00
Benedict Warren & Davidson Co.; Memphis, TN	$16.00
Bengall; England	$8.00
Benitz, Leo C.; Philadelphia, PA	$12.00
Bennett; England	$10.00
Beringhaus, Eugene & Co.; Cincinnati, OH	$11.00
Best Steel; England	$9.00
B'Ham Barber Supply Co.; CA	$8.00
Biglein; England	$11.00
Biglow & Dowse Co.; Germany	$10.00
Bingham, C.T.; England	$11.00
Bingham, James; England	$12.00
Bingham W., Co.; Cleveland, OH	$14.00
Binghampton Cutlery Co.; Binghampton, NY	$11.00
Birks, M.; England	$8.00
Birks, Wm. & John; England	$8.00

Birmingham Barber Supply Co.; Birmingham, AL	$14.00
Bisby & Co.; England	$10.00
Bishop Co.; Cleveland, OH	$10.00
Bishop & Sons; OH	$12.00
Bismark Razor Works; Germany	$11.00
Bison Mfg.; Little Valley, NY	$18.00
B.K. Company (Trademark-NSEY); WV	$9.00
B & L; OH	$9.00
Black Diamond Cutlery; Germany/NY	$14.00
Black, Ross W.; Pittsburgh, PA	$10.00
Blackman, Phillip; Germany	$10.00
Blackwell, Alfred; England	$11.00
Blehl, Edward; Washington D.C.	$12.00
Blue Steel; Germany	$10.00
Bocker, Fredrick; Germany	$10.00
Boivin; France	$12.00
* Boker, Henri & Co.; Germany	$12.00

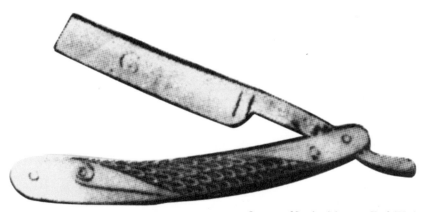

Courtesy of Smokey Mountain Knife Works

(a) Brand and Origin Base Value	(b) Handle Material % Value	(c) Artwork % Value	(d) Condition % Value	(e) Collector Value
H. Boker & Co. Germany **$12.00**	Ivory Celluloid 12 x 300%= **$36.00**	High relief carving 12 x 400%= **$48.00**	Collectible **100%**	$36 + $48 =$84 $84 x 100%= **$84.00**

49

Bolka, A & K; Finland	$8.00
Bonham, L.C.; El Paso, TX	$11.00
Bonita; Germany	$10.00
Boots; England	$11.00
Boss; Toledo, OH	$14.00
Bossif, Alley & Bros.; Pennsylvania	$10.00
Bossing Razor Co.; Providence, RI	$11.00
Bosswick, A.; Ohio	$10.00
Bostwick Braun Co.; Toledo, Ohio	$10.00
Boucher; USA	$6.00
* Bourdlabbe; Paris, France	$12.00

Courtesy of Smokey Mountain Knife Works

(a) Brand and Origin Base Value	(b) Handle Material % Value	(c) Artwork % Value	(d) Condition % Value	(e) Collector Value
Bourdlabbe Paris, France **$12.00**	Black Composition 12 x 150%= **$18.00**	Nonexistent **0**	Excellent **200%**	$18 + 0 =$18 $18 x 200%= **$36.00**

Bouvier Laboratories, Inc.; USA	$10.00
Bowins Art; MN	$11.00
Bowdins Barber & Tools; USA	$10.00
Bradley Bros.; USA	$10.00
Bradonia Cutlery Co.; Germany	$10.00
Brandt, M.L. Cutlery; NY/Germany	$10.00
Brandtford Cutlery Co.; USA	$11.00
Bresduck, NY	$9.00
Bresnick; NY	$12.00
Bresnick, B.S.; Germany	$9.00
* Bresnick, C.S.; Germany	$10.00
Brick, F.; England	$9.00
Bridge Cutlery Co.; St. Louis, MO	$22.00

Courtesy of Smokey Mountain Knife Works

(a) Brand and Origin Base Value	(b) Handle Material % Value	(c) Artwork % Value	(d) Condition % Value	(e) Collector Value
C.S. Bresnick Germany **$10.00**	Slick Black Composition 10 x 150%= **$15.00**	Grim Reaper bolsters 15 x 200%= **$30.00**	Good **150%**	$15 + $30=$45 $45 x 150%= $67.50 **$68.00**

Briggs & Spencer; England	$12.00
Bright, Fred W.	$9.00
Brikendahl, C & H; USA	$11.00
Brint, Hall, Lamb & Co.; England	$12.00
Bris, T.G., WV	$10.00
Brittain, Wilkinson & Brownell; England	$11.00
Broadway Cutlery Co.; Germany	$10.00
Broeker, Fredrick; Elizabeth, NJ/Germany	$10.00
Brookes & Crookes; England	$10.00
Brown Camp Hardware; USA	$12.00
Brown, John; IL	$11.00
Bruff Bros. & Seaver; England	$12.00
Buck Brothers; USA	$12.00
Buckeye Barber Supply Co.; OH	$12.00
* Buerger Bros. Supply Co.;	
Pueblo & Denver CO, Des Moines, IA	$10.00
Burgess Hardware Co.; USA	$9.00
Burlington Barber Supply House; USA	$10.00
Burnham & Fehr. Barber Supply; Germany	$10.00
Burrell Cutlery Co; Ellicottville, NY	$12.00
Buss, Henry & Son(s); NY	$10.00
Butcher, W. & Son; England	$12.00
Butler, George & Son; England	$11.00
Cadmen, David; England	$9.00

Courtesy of the Dewey Whited Collection

(a) Brand and Origin Base Value	(b) Handle Material % Value	(c) Artwork % Value	(d) Condition % Value	(e) Collector Value
Buerger Bros. Supply Co. **$10.00**	Black Horn 10 x 150%= **$15.00**	Nonexistent **0**	Collectible- **85%**	$15 + 0=$15 $15 x 85%= $12.75 **$13.00**

Cadman, Luke; England	$9.00
Cadman & Sons; England	$9.00
California Notions and Toy Co.; CA	$8.00
California Tool & Cut. Co.; CA	$15.00
Caldwell, A.B. Mfg. Co.; IN	$10.00
Calle & Prez	$8.00
Calvin, Nicholas B.	$8.00
Cam, Joseph	$7.00
Cambridge Barber Supply Co.; OH	$10.00
Camco; NY	$15.00+
Camillus Cutlery; NY	$20.00+
Cammell-Laird & Co.; Germany	$10.00
Campbell Co., H.D.; England	$10.00
Campbell, R.D.; USA	$11.00
Canton-Akron Barber Supply Co.; OH	$14.00
* Canton Cutlery Co.; Canton, OH	$9.00
Capitol Cut. Co.; NY	$13.00
Cargill, T.S.	$10.00
Carlsbad Razor; Nashville, TN	$14.00
Carlson-Lusk, ID	$14.00
Carmen Razor; Germany	$10.00
Caroboolad, C.; OH	$8.00

Courtesy of Smokey Mountain Knife Works

(a) Brand and Origin Base Value	(b) Handle Material % Value	(c) Artwork % Value	(d) Condition % Value	(e) Collector Value
Canton Cutlery Co. Canton, OH **$9.00**	Celluloid 9 x 300%= **$27.00**	Personalized + picture of horse & bird dog on handle 9 x 200%= **$18.00**	Collectible **100%**	$27 + $18=$45 $45 x 100%= **$45.00**

Carroll Cutlery & Co., Chicago	$10.00
∗ Case, Ace; Bradford, PA	$30.00
∗ Case Brothers; Spring Valley, NY	$40.00
Case Mfg. Co.; Little Valley, NY	$35.00
∗ Case, W.R. & Sons; Bradford, PA	$30.00
Case, W.R., Tested	$30.00

Courtesy of the Dewey Whited Collection

(a) Brand and Origin Base Value	(b) Handle Material % Value	(c) Artwork % Value	(d) Condition % Value	(e) Collector Value
Cases's "Ace" Bradford, PA **$30.00**	Celluloid 30 x 275%= $82.50 **$83.00**	Interesting handles 30 x 200%= **$60.00**	Collectible- **80%**	$83+$60=$143 $143 x 80%= $114.40 **$114.00**

Courtesy of the Dewey Whited Collection

(a) Brand and Origin Base Value	(b) Handle Material % Value	(c) Artwork % Value	(d) Condition % Value	(e) Collector Value
Case Bros. Spring Valley, NY **$40.00**	Slick Black 40 x 150%= **$60.00**	Strap bolsters 40 x 200%= **$80.00**	Collectible **100%**	$60+$80=$140 $140 x 100%= **$140.00**

Courtesy of Smokey Mountain Knife Works

(a) Brand and Origin Base Value	(b) Handle Material % Value	(c) Artwork % Value	(d) Condition % Value	(e) Collector Value
W.R. Case & Sons Bradford, PA **$20.00**	Clear Green Celluloid 20 x 300%= **$60.00**	Colorful 20 x 100%= **$20.00**	Collectible **100%**	$60 + $20=$80 $80 x 100%= **$80.00**

Cassel, Fred	$7.00
Cast Steel; England	$7.00
* Cattaraugus Cutlery Co.; Little Valley, NY	$28.00
CCC (Cleveland Cutlery Co.); Germany	$14.00
CCC (Curtin & Clark Cutlery Co.); Kansas City, MO	$20.00
C. & D.H. Co.; NY	$11.00
Centaur; OH	$11.00
Century, 20th Mfg. Co.; IL	$12.00
C. F. & R.; Portland, OR	$10.00
Chaffee & Blackburn; MI	$9.00
Challenge Cutlery Co.; England	$13.00
Challenge Cutlery Co.; Bridegeport, CT	$30.00+
Challenge Razor Co.; CT	$25.00+
Champaign Barber Supply; IL	$10.00

Courtesy of Smokey Mountain Knife Works

(a) Brand and Origin Base Value	(b) Handle Material % Value	(c) Artwork % Value	(d) Condition % Value	(e) Collector Value
Cattaraugus Cutlery Co. Little Valley, NY **$28.00**	Ivory Celluloid 28 x 300%= **$84.00**	Fancy bol- sters, Indian head inlay 28 x 325%= **$91.00**	Collectible **100%**	$84+$91=$175 $175 x 100%= **$175.00**

Champion, Thomas & Son; England	$10.00+
Champlin, J.B.; England	$11.00+
Charlton; England	$11.00
Chesi, Ascoli, Piceno; Italy	$12.00
Chicago Mail Order Co.; Germany	$11.00
Chicago Pocket Knife Co.; Chicago, IL	$12.00
Child, Pratt & Co.	$12.00
Chip-A-Way Cutlery; England	$14.00
Cholwell, George R.; England	$10.00
Chores, James; England	$8.00
Chrisian (cast steel); England	$10.00
Christ, Hacker; OH	$10.00
Christensen, H.M.; MA	$12.00
Christofferson; MN	$10.00
Christy Co.; Freemont, OH	$15.00
Church & Morse; USA	$11.00
Clancy, R.; Boston, MA	$10.00
Clar, John & Sons; England	$10.00
Clarice & Son, John; England	$10.00
Clark, Bob; England	$8.00
Clark Bros.; England	$10.00+
Clark Bros. Co.; Germany	$10.00+
Clark Warranted; England	$7.00
* Clark & Hall Warranted; England	$10.00

Courtesy of Smokey Mountain Knife Works

(a) Brand and Origin Base Value	(b) Handle Material % Value	(c) Artwork % Value	(d) Condition % Value	(e) Collector Value
Clark & Hall Warranted England **$10.00**	Horn 10 x 275%= $27.50 **$28.00**	Nonexistent **0**	Some handle damage Collectible- 75%	$28 + 0 = $28 $28 x 75%= **$21.00**

Classic; USA	$10.00
Clauberg & Co.; Germany	$8.00
Claubery & Co., F.A.; NY/Germany	$9.00
Clauss; Fremont, OH	$14.00
Clauss, Henrie; OH	$15.00
Clauss Shear Works; USA	$17.00
Clayton, John Shaw (cast steel); OH	$11.00
Cleff, Vom & Co.; NY	$11.00
Clement, Charles; England	$9.00
Clements, Joseph; England	$8.00
Clemmson's	$10.00
Cleveland Cut. Co.; OH	$10.00
* Clifford Hwd. Co.; Evansville, IN	$10.00

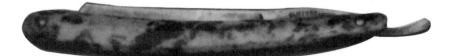

Courtesy of Smokey Mountain Knife Works

(a) Brand and Origin Base Value	(b) Handle Material % Value	(c) Artwork % Value	(d) Condition % Value	(e) Collector Value
Clifford Hwd. Co. Evansville, IN **$10.00**	Yellow & Brown Cellu- loid/Mottled 10 x 300%= **$30.00**	Beautiful handles 10 x 150%= **$15.00**	Collectible **100%**	$30 + $15=$45 $45 x 100%= **$45.00**

Clifford Co.; ME	$10.00
Clisten Razor Mfg. Co.; NY	$11.00
Clyde Steelworks; OH	$12.00
Coch & Shaver; Germany	$8.00
Cockhill Co., John; England	$10.00
Coe, John G.; England	$9.00
Cohen, S.S.; NJ	$10.00
Colguhoun & Cadman; England	$10.00
Colibri; France	$12.00
Colishaw, Wm.; England	$10.00
Collette, A.; England	$11.00
Collins, T.C.; CT	$12.00
Collister, David H. Co.; OH	$11.00
Colly & Co.; England	$8.00
Colman, Breg; USA	$11.00
Colonial Razor; Germany	$10.00
Colonial Steel Co.; PA	$12.00
* Columbia Cutlery Co.; Worcester, MA	$14.00

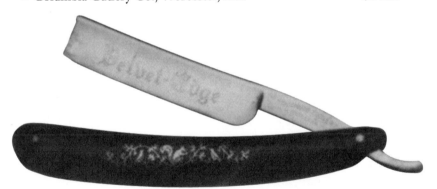

Courtesy of Smokey Mountain Knife Works

(a) Brand and Origin Base Value	(b) Handle Material % Value	(c) Artwork % Value	(d) Condition % Value	(e) Collector Value
Columbia Cutlery Co. Worcester, MA **$14.00**	Slick Black Composition 14 x 150%= **$21.00**	Blade etch & handle inlay of bird & squirrel 14 x 200%= **$28.00**	Collectible **100%**	$21 + $28=$49 $49 x 100%= **$49.00**

Columbus Hdw.; OH	$14.00
Colvolt & Smith; PA	$11.00
Compton, W.H.; NJ	$8.00
Congreaves Works; England	$10.00
Congreve's, C.; England	$10.00
Connecticut Cutlery Co.; CT	$10.00+
Constanin, M.J.; PA	$9.00
* Continental Cutlery Co.; England/Germany	$15.00

Courtesy of Smokey Mountain Knife Works

(a) Brand and Origin Base Value	(b) Handle Material % Value	(c) Artwork % Value	(d) Condition % Value	(e) Collector Value
Continental Cutlery Co. Germany **$15.00**	3-piece Genuine Pearl 15 x 400%= **$60.00**	Blade etch of T. Roosevelt 15 x 300%= **$45.00**	Good **150%**	$60+$45=$105 $105 x 150%= $157.50 **$158.00**

Cook, Everette & Pennell; Germany	$12.00
Cooper Bros.; England	$9.00
Copley J. & Sons; England	$10.00
Coppel, Alexander; England	$10.00
Corby, J.F. & Co.; IL	$10.00
Corn, O.W.; Little Valley, NY	$25.00
Corrado, O.; Chicago, IL	$11.00
Cosmo Mfg. Co.; Germany	$9.00
Cosmopolitan, Jay	$9.00
Costa & Sons; MA	$8.00
* Coualt & Smith; Pittsburgh, PA	$11.00

Courtesy of Smokey Mountain Knife Works

(a) Brand and Origin Base Value	(b) Handle Material % Value	(c) Artwork % Value	(d) Condition % Value	(e) Collector Value
Coualt & Smith Pittsburgh, PA **$11.00**	Slick Black Composition 11 x 150%= $16.50 **$17.00**	Fancy bolster of boy & girl 11 x 200%= **$22.00**	Collectible **100%**	$17 + $22=$39 $39 x 100%= **$39.00**

Coudert, J.A.; Paris, France	$13.00
Coulson, John; England	$10.00
Couptiel; England	$8.00
Courtice; England	$10.00
Coy & Co.; England	$7.00
Cracker Jack; Siam	$12.00
* Crandal Cutlery Co.; Bradford, PA	$20.00

Courtesy of Smokey Mountain Knife Works

(a) Brand and Origin Base Value	(b) Handle Material % Value	(c) Artwork % Value	(d) Condition % Value	(e) Collector Value
Crandal Cutlery Co. Bradford, PA **$20.00**	Plain Black Composition 20 x 150%= **$30.00**	Nonexistent **0**	Excellent **200%**	$30 + 0 = $30 $30 x 200%= **$60.00**

Crane Cutlery Co.; NY, USA	$25.00
Cranford Razor Works; Cranford, NJ	$20.00
Crater Razor Co.; Columbus, OH	$12.00
Crawshaw, James; England	$11.00
* Creal, J.H.; Upton, KY	$14.00
Crescent Razor Co.; IL	$13.00
Cress Mfg. Co.; PA	$10.00
Creswick, John; England	$10.00
Croghan Cut. Co.; Ohio	$10.00

Courtesy of Smokey Mountain Knife Works

(a) Brand and Origin Base Value	(b) Handle Material % Value	(c) Artwork % Value	(d) Condition % Value	(e) Collector Value
J.H. Creal Upton, KY **$14.00**	Fancy Candy Stripe 14 x 300%= **$42.00**	Blade etch worked handles 14 x 300%= **$42.00**	Collectible **100%**	$42 + $42=$84 $84 x 100%= **$84.00**

Croisdale, Leeds; England	$10.00
Crookes, G. & Co.; England	$12.00
Crookes, John; England	$12.00
Crown Cutlery; Germany/NY	$10.00
Crown Razor; Boston, MA	$12.00
* Crown & Sword Razor Works; Germany	$9.00

Courtesy of Smokey Mountain Knife Works

(a) Brand and Origin Base Value	(b) Handle Material % Value	(c) Artwork % Value	(d) Condition % Value	(e) Collector Value
Crown & Sword Razor Works Germany **$9.00**	Ivory Celluloid 9 x 300%= **$27.00**	Nude with rose 9 x 450%= $40.50 **$41.00**	Good **150%**	$27 + $41=$68 $68 x 150%= **$102.00**

Cruse & Behman Hwd.; OH	$14.00
Cuddack, R.W.; Corning, NY	$10.00
Culf & Kay; England	$12.00
Curcia & Co., J.V.; NJ	$8.00
Curcio Barber Supply Co.; NJ	$8.00
* Curley's; NY	$11.00

Courtesy of Smokey Mountain Knife Works

(a) Brand and Origin Base Value	(b) Handle Material % Value	(c) Artwork % Value	(d) Condition % Value	(e) Collector Value
Curley's Easy-Shaving Safety Razor NY **$11.00**	White Composition 11 x 150%= $16.50 **$17.00**	Inlay & advertising 11 x 200%= **$22.00**	Blade nicked Collectible- **85%**	$17 + $22=$39 $39 x 85%= $33.15 **$33.00**

Currie Co.; NJ	$10.00
Curten, W.; Germany	$9.00
Cuso, John Hudson	$10.00
Cuswa & Bro., H.T.	$9.00
Cuter Hardware Co.	$9.00
Cuterix; Germany	$8.00
Cuterly Associates; NY	$25.00
Cutler Hardin Co.	$10.00
Cywon, A. Barber Supply Co.; Germany	$9.00
Dahlgren, C.W.; Sweden	$12.00
Damann & Co., Ernst; Germany	$9.00
Damascara; Fremont, OH	$13.00
Damascus Razor; England	$10.00
Dame, Stoddard & Kendall; Boston, MA	$10.00
D'ARCY & Co., John; Germany	$9.00
David & Rizk Co.; Germany	$9.00
Davis, E.M. Co., IL	$12.00
Dawes & Ball; England	$10.00
Dayton Barber Supply Co.; Dayton, OH	$11.00
D & B (Dorescher & Behar); NY/Germany	$10.00
Des Moines Barber Supply; Des Moines, IA	$11.00
Dennison Barber Supply; TX	$11.00

De Pews; NY	$8.00
DeVry Barber Supply Co.; IN	$9.00
De Wolfe & Vincent; Germany	$10.00
Deakin & Sons, George; England	$9.00
Dealer's Sales Corp.; USA/Germany	$9.00
Delp & Rossler	$8.00
Denison Barber Supply Co.; TX	$10.00
Dery Barber Supply Co.; IN	$10.00
Desco Dealer's Sales Corp.; Germany	$9.00
Deutsch, Otto & Sohne; Germany	$10.00
Deutzmann, Hugo	$10.00
Devon Mfg. Co.; Germany	$10.00
Dewey Razor Co.	$12.00
Dewsnap, Francis; Germany	$9.00
Diamond Edge, (Shapleigh); St. Louis, MO	$22.00
Diamond Razor Co.; IN	$14.00
Diamond Spear; Germany	$11.00
Diamondine; Germany	$10.00
Diane; Japan	$10.00
Dickson, C.M.; Sioux City, IA	$15.00
Dilsworth; NJ/PA	$10.00
Discobolo; Germany	$9.00
Dixie Manufacturing Co.; GA	$14.00
Dixon Cutlery Co.; Germany	$10.00
D.K.S.; Japan	$10.00
D.M.A.; Germany	$9.00
Dobie, J.	$9.00
Doctor Scott's Electric	$9.00
Dodd, J. C.; England	$9.00
Doddozu	$9.00
Dodges, N. & R.; England	$9.00
Dolle, Fred; Chicago; IL	$10.00
Donner, H. & Co.	$10.00
Donvan, J.W. Co.; MA	$11.00

Dorechester & Behar; Germany	$9.00
DORKO; Germany	$10.00
Dorlot, Belle-Ile; France	$11.00
Dotzert, J.H.; WA	$10.00
Driefuss; Germany	$11.00
Droescher, S.R., Inc.; NY/Germany	$8.00
D. S. & K. (Dame, Stoddard & Kenndall); Germany/Boston	$10.00
Dubl Duck; Germany	$12.00
Dubreul, Renadt; France	$10.00
Dunlap, J. & Co.; NY	$10.00
Dunne, James H., & Co.; Boston	$11.00
Duranta U.; Germany	$9.00
Durham Duplex; Jersey City, NJ	$6.00
Eagle Hardware Co.; Germany	$10.00
East St. Louis Barber Supply Co.; East St. Louis, IL	$9.00
Eastern Cut. Co.; NY	$12.00
Eclipse Cutlery Co.; Germany	$10.00
E. DACO Darmann & Co.	$10.00
Eddy Mfg. Co.; ME	$12.00
Edlis Barber Supply Co.; Pittsburgh, PA	$9.00
Edwards; Germany	$9.00
Edwards, Robert; England	$11.00
Edwards & Walker Hardware Co.; Portland, ME	$12.00
E. G. Co.; England	$10.00
Ehle & Hagemann	$9.00
Eichoff, A. & Co.; NY	$10.00
Eickinson, E.; England	$9.00
Eickler, H. & Shonne; Germany	$9.00
Eigenbord, W.; Germany	$9.00
Einbeck, August	$9.00
Eisemann, P.; PA/Germany	$10.00
Ek-Seb	$12.00
E. & L. Co.; MD	$9.00
Electric Cutlery Co.; NY	$14.00

Electro Boracic	$10.00
Elgin-American Mfg Co.; USA (IL?)	$16.00
Elias & Aboussleman; NY	$10.00
Elias, Salim; NY	$11.00
Elin, Thomas & Co.; England	$11.00
** Elliot, Joseph; England	$11.00

Courtesy of Smokey Mountain Knife Works

(a) Brand and Origin Base Value	(b) Handle Material % Value	(c) Artwork % Value	(d) Condition % Value	(e) Collector Value
Joseph Elliot England **$11.00**	Imitation Ivory 11 x 150%= $16.50 **$17.00**	Fancy crown bolsters 11 x 200%= **$22.00**	Collectible **100%**	$17 + $22=$39 $39 x 100%= **$39.00**

Courtesy of the Dewey Whited Collection

(a) Brand and Origin Base Value	(b) Handle Material % Value	(c) Artwork % Value	(d) Condition % Value	(e) Collector Value
Joseph Elliot England **$11.00**	Ivory Celluloid 11 x 300%= **$33.00**	Nonexistent **0**	Collectible **100%**	$33 + 0=$33 $33 x 100%= **$33.00**

Elliot, William; England	$12.00
* Elliot, William and Co.; Germany	$10.00
Elliott, John; England	$10.00
Ellis, Edwin N.; Germany	$10.00
Ellwanger, A.H.; Philadelphia	$12.00
Elrick, A., Cutlery; England	$12.00

Courtesy of Smokey Mountain Knife Works

(a) Brand and Origin Base Value	(b) Handle Material % Value	(c) Artwork % Value	(d) Condition % Value	(e) Collector Value
Wm. Elliot & Co. Germany **$10.00**	Slick Black Composition 10 x 150%= **$15.00**	Inland w/ pearl & abolone in a floral design 10 x 300%= **$30.00**	Collectible **100%**	$15 + $30=$45 $45 x 100%= **$45.00**

Elsener; Switzerland	$11.00
Emblem Razor Co.; NY	$12.00
Empire Barber Supply Co.; Philadelphia, PA	$17.00
Empire Knife Co.; CT	$20.00
Empire Razor Co.; Winsted, CT	$20.00
Emrich, P.; Cincinnati, OH	$10.00
Emrich, H.E.; OH	$9.00
Emue Bros; Germany	$9.00
Enderes Inc.; MN	$10.00
Enders, W.; MO	$10.00
Engels, C.W.; NY/Germany	$10.00
Engles, Karl & Son	$10.00
Engström, John; NY/Sweden	$18.00
Enterprise Cut Co.; St. Louis, MO	$16.00
** ERN; Germany	$11.00
Ernesto; Germany	$9.00
Ernst, L. & Sons; NY	$9.00
Etty Mfg. Co; Worcester, MA	$10.00
Ewald, Plumacher	$9.00
Excelsior Cutlery Co.; Germany/NY	$14.00
Eyewitness; Germany	$12.00
* Eyre, B.J.; England	$12.00

Courtesy of Smokey Mountain Knife Works

(a) Brand and Origin Base Value	(b) Handle Material % Value	(c) Artwork % Value	(d) Condition % Value	(e) Collector Value
ERN Germany **$11.00**	Ivory Celluloid 11 x 300%= **$33.00**	Crown & sword relief + windmill & farm screen "Ornate" 11 x 550%= $60.50 **$61.00**	Good **150%**	$33 + $61=$94 $94 x 150%= **$141.00**

Courtesy of Smokey Mountain Knife Works

(a) Brand and Origin Base Value	(b) Handle Material % Value	(c) Artwork % Value	(d) Condition % Value	(e) Collector Value
ERN Germany **$11.00**	Ivory Celluloid 11 x 300%= **$33.00**	Standing nude w/ flora, hand coloring on handles 11 x 500%= **$55.00**	Good **150%**	$33 + $55=$88 $88 x 150%= **$132.00**

Courtesy of the Dewey Whited Collection

(a) Brand and Origin Base Value	(b) Handle Material % Value	(c) Artwork % Value	(d) Condition % Value	(e) Collector Value
B.J. Eyre England **$12.00**	Horn-Black 12 x 200%= **$24.00**	Etched blade 12 x 100%= **$12.00**	Collectible- **90%**	$24 + $12=$36 $36 x 90%= $32.40 **$32.00**

Faber, John; Germany	$10.00
Fabyan Knife Co.; Germany	$9.00
F.A.F. Mfg. & Import Co.; NE	$11.00
Faour, D.J. & Bros.	$10.00
Faroh; England	$10.00
Fascination; England	$10.00
* Faultless; Germany	$10.00

Courtesy of Smokey Mountain Knife Works

(a) Brand and Origin Base Value	(b) Handle Material % Value	(c) Artwork % Value	(d) Condition % Value	(e) Collector Value
Faultless Germany **$10.00**	Cast Aluminum 10 x 350%= **$35.00**	Sea maiden nude (front) alligator (bk) 10 x 550%= **$55.00**	Collectible **100%**	$35 + $55=$90 $90 x 100%= **$90.00**

Fawn Supply Co.; Chicago, IL	$9.00
* F&B; Germany	$15.00
Feist, Joseph; Germany	$10.00
Felix, Gustav	$9.00
Felt Pad Razor Works; St. Louis, MO	$11.00

Courtesy of Smokey Mountain Knife Works

(a) Brand and Origin Base Value	(b) Handle Material % Value	(c) Artwork % Value	(d) Condition % Value	(e) Collector Value
F & B Germany **$15.00**	Sterling Silver 15 x 500%= **$75.00**	Die struck high relief 15 x 550%= $82.50 **$83.00**	Good **150%**	$75+$83=$158 $158 x 150%= **$237.00**

Listings of Companies & Base Values

Feltus Bros.; MS		$14.00
* Fenney, Fredrick (Tally-Ho Razor); England		$16.00

Courtesy of Smokey Mountain Knife Works

(a) Brand and Origin Base Value	(b) Handle Material % Value	(c) Artwork % Value	(d) Condition % Value	(e) Collector Value
F. Fenny "Tally-Ho Razor" England **$16.00**	Genuine Stag 16 x 400%= **$64.00**	Bar shield/ blade etch 16 x 200%= **$32.00**	Collectible+ **125%**	$64 + $32=$96 $96 x 125%= **$120.00**

Fenton, Joseph & Sons; England		$10.00
Feoriere, P.F.		$10.00
Fermarud		$9.00
F & F Special		$10.00
Field, Alfred & Co.; NY/England/Germany		$12.00
* Fielder, T.J. & Sons; Springfield, MO		$10.00

Courtesy of Smokey Mountain Knife Works

(a) Brand and Origin Base Value	(b) Handle Material % Value	(c) Artwork % Value	(d) Condition % Value	(e) Collector Value
T.J. Fielder Springfield, MO **$10.00**	Yellow Celluloid 10 x 300%= **$30.00**	Silver inlay 10 x 200%= **$20.00**	Excellent **200%**	$30 + $20=$50 $50 x 200%= **$100.00**

Finedge Cutlery Corp.; NY		$20.00
Fione, India Steel Razor		$10.00
Fiox Cutlery Co.; Germany		$11.00
Fisco Razor Werke; Germany		$10.00

Fisher, H.; England		$10.00
* Flagg, J.H. Cutlery Co. Ltd.; NY/England/France		$12.00

Courtesy of Smokey Mountain Knife Works

(a) Brand and Origin Base Value	(b) Handle Material % Value	(c) Artwork % Value	(d) Condition % Value	(e) Collector Value
James H. Flagg France, USA Patten 1899 **$12.00**	Black Composition 12 x 150%= **$18.00**	Extra long "Monkey Tail" 12 x 300%= **$36.00**	Good **150%**	$18 + $36=$54 $54 x 150%= **$81.00**

Floyd & Bohr Co.; KY	$12.00
Flynn; Omaha, NE	$10.00
Foery & Bauer; NY	$8.00
Folis Barber Supply Co.; PA	$10.00
Fontenille Medaille; Argentina	$13.00
Foote & Shear Co.	$9.00
Ford & Medley; England	$10.00
Fort Worth Barber Supply; Fort Worth, TX	$11.00
Forzy, G. & Co.; England	$13.00
Fos, Hugh & Co.	$9.00
Fossum, B.B.	$9.00
Foster & Bailey	$9.00
Foster, Theo & Brothers; Fulton, NY	$9.00
Fox Cutlery; Germany	$8.00
Fox & Norris	$9.00
Fox, Wm.	$10.00
Frank's Barber Supply; TX	$11.00
Franklin Cutlery; Germany	$9.00
Franklin Razor Co.; Philadelphia, PA	$12.00
Franz, F. & Sons; Boston, MA	$12.00
Frederick's (Celebrated Razor) Co.; England	$12.00
Fretwil, Thomas & Son; England	$10.00

Friedmann & Lauterjung; NY	$11.00
Fri-Ko; Germany	$10.00
Fromm, Otto Cutlery; Germany/NY	$12.00
Frost, Peter Co.; Chicago	$15.00
Fuller Morrison Co.; Chicago, IL	$10.00
Fulton Cutlery Co.; NY	$12.00
Furniss Cutlery; England	$11.00
Gambert, H.; NY	$10.00
* Ganem, Hnos, Monterey & Torreon; USA	$9.00

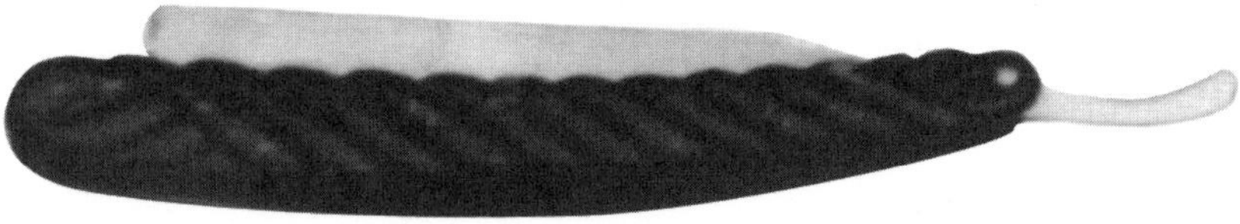

Courtesy of Smokey Mountain Knife Works

(a) Brand and Origin Base Value	(b) Handle Material % Value	(c) Artwork % Value	(d) Condition % Value	(e) Collector Value
Ganem, Hnos Monterey & Torreon USA **$9.00**	Multicolored twist 9 x 150%= $13.50 **$14.00**	Blade etching of 3 U.S. Presidents 9 x 400%= **$36.00**	Good **150%**	$14 + $36=$50 $50 x 150%= **$75.00**

Gans, Wm.	$9.00
* Garibaldi, Gppe; Italy	$10.00
Garland Cutlery Co.; Germany	$10.00
Garnier, Paris	$10.00
Garrett, J.M. Barber Supply; Kansas City, MO	$9.00
Gay, W. & Sons	$9.00
G.C. Co.; NY	$10.00
Gebruder Rauh Grafath; Germany	$9.00
Geebe Hardware Co., Frank	$8.00
Geissen, D.E. & Co.; OH	$9.00
Geldmacher, Gebert; Germany	$9.00
Geller, Ward & Hasner Hardware Co.; St. Louis, MO	$18.00
Gelwan; New Jersey/Germany	$10.00
Gem Cutlery Co.; NY	$11.00

Courtesy of Smokey Mountain Knife Works

(a) Brand and Origin Base Value	(b) Handle Material % Value	(c) Artwork % Value	(d) Condition % Value	(e) Collector Value
Gppe. Garibaldi Italy **$10.00**	Slick Black 10 x 150%= **$15.00**	Pewter framed picture on handle 10 x 350%= **$35.00**	Chip on handle Collectible- **75%**	$15 + $35=$50 $50 x 75%= $37.50 **$38.00**

★ Genco Co.; Bradford, PA	$15.00
Geneva Cutlery Co.; Geneva, NY	$11.00
George, John L.	$9.00
George, L.M.	$9.00
George & Son; Germany	$10.00
Gerbr, Bell; Germany	$10.00
Germania Cutlery Works; Germany	$11.00
Gerry, C.P.; England	$10.00
Gesse n. Vda Esparteros G.; Madrid, Spain	$12.00
Gevoso; Germany	$9.00
GiBi	$9.00
Giesen & Frosthoff; Germany	$10.00

Courtesy of Smokey Mountain Knife Works

(a) Brand and Origin Base Value	(b) Handle Material % Value	(c) Artwork % Value	(d) Condition % Value	(e) Collector Value
Genco Co. "Old Dutch Razor" **$15.00**	Plastic 15 x 100%= **$15.00**	Nonexistent **0**	Excellent **150%**	$15 + 0 = $15 $15 x 150%= $22.50 **$23.00**

Giessen, D.E. Co.; Cleveland, OH	$10.00
Giesser, Chas. P.; Buffalo, NY	$9.00
Gilbert & Sons	$9.00
Gilchrist, Wm.; NJ & Philadelphia	$20.00
Gilert Sevillewerks; Germany	$9.00
Gillam & Spetnagel; Chillicothe, OH	$10.00
Gilsdorf's; Germany	$8.00
Ginnard, Charles; CT/Germany	$12.00
Glesen & Forsthoff; Germany	$10.00
* Goar, Harris Mfg. Co.; Kansas City, MO	$10.00

Courtesy of the Dewey Whited Collection

(a) Brand and Origin Base Value	(b) Handle Material % Value	(c) Artwork % Value	(d) Condition % Value	(e) Collector Value
Goar, Harris Co. Kansas City, MO **$10.00**	Slick Black 10 x 150%= **$15.00**	Blade etch 10 x 75%= $7.50 **$8.00**	Collectible **100%**	$15 + $8=$23 $23 x 100%= **$23.00**

Gold	$10.00
Gold Bug (Crown Razor Co.); NY	$12.00
Gold Metal; Lincoln, NE	$12.00
* Golden Rule Cutlery (G.R.C.Co.); Chicago, IL	$11.00

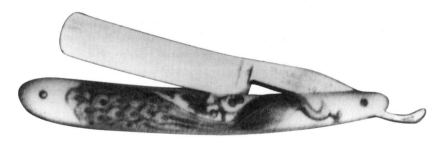

Courtesy of Smokey Mountain Knife Works

(a) Brand and Origin Base Value	(b) Handle Material % Value	(c) Artwork % Value	(d) Condition % Value	(e) Collector Value
Golden Rule Cutlery Chicago, IL **$11.00**	Ivory Celluloid 11 x 300%= **$33.00**	Detailed relief of col- ored peacock 11 x 550%= $60.50 **$61.00**	Good **150%**	$33 + $61=$94 $94 x 150%= **$141.00**

Goldey Bros., Inc.; Cincinnati, OH	$9.00
Golf Brand; Germany	$9.00
Gordon & Son	$10.00
Gould, Muerinder	$9.00
Gould, W.	$9.00
Gradwell; England	$10.00
Graef & Schmidt; Germany/NY	$12.00
Grafin Cutlery; Columbus, PA	$12.00
Grah, Charles G. (Hoosier Razor); Indianapolis, IN/Germany	$10.00
Grah & Plumacher (Blue Diamond); Germany	$14.00
Grant, Daniel; England	$9.00
Gratian Cast Steel	$10.00
Gratin, Jonathan; England	$10.00
Graves, Henry Razor Co.; Canadaiqua, NY	$9.00
Gray & Dudley Hardware Co.; Nashville/Germany	$12.00
* Greaves, W. & Son Sheaf Works; England	$20.00
Greaves, Wm.; England	$18.00
* Greaves, W. & Sons; England/Holland	$17.00
Green, James G.	$8.00
Green, Pickslay & Appleby; England	$10.00
Gresh, V.; Toledo, OH	$9.00
Grevemeyer, W.H. & Co.; Philadelphia	$9.00
Grieb, Bros.	$9.00
Grieb, Charles	$8.00
Griffin Cutlery Works; NY/Germany	$12.00
Griffon Cutlery Works; England	$11.00

Courtesy of the Dewey Whited Collection

(a) Brand and Origin Base Value	(b) Handle Material % Value	(c) Artwork % Value	(d) Condition % Value	(e) Collector Value
W. Greaves & Son Sheaf Works England **$17.00**	Clear horn 17 x 275%= $46.75 **$47.00**	Nonexistent **0**	Well worn Collectible- **75%**	$47 + 0=$47 $47 x 75%= $35.25 **$35.00**

Courtesy of Smokey Mountain Knife Works

(a) Brand and Origin Base Value	(b) Handle Material % Value	(c) Artwork % Value	(d) Condition % Value	(e) Collector Value
W. Greaves & Sons England **$20.00**	German Stag 20 x 400%= **$80.00**	Bar shield & old style blade knotch 20 x 150%= **$30.00**	Good **150%**	$80+$30=$110 $110 x 150%= **$165.00**

* Griffon XX; Germany	$9.00
Grinding, H.H. & Co.; Cleveland, OH	$12.00
Groesbreck & Co.; New York City	$11.00
Groescher, S.R., Inc.; NY	$9.00
G.R.S.; Germany	$8.00
Guarantee Barber Supply; Philadelphia/Germany	$10.00
Guarantee Cutlery Co.; NY	$12.00
Gullant Razor Co.; Atlanta, GA	$12.00
Gunkel Barber Supply Co.; St. Louis, MO	$9.00
Gunn Tool & Supply Co.; Pittsburgh, PA	$12.00

Courtesy of the Dewey Whited Collection

(a) Brand and Origin Base Value	(b) Handle Material % Value	(c) Artwork % Value	(d) Condition % Value	(e) Collector Value
Griffon XX Germany **$9.00**	Horn-Black 9 x 150%= $13.50 **$14.00**	Nonexistent **0**	Good **150%**	$14 + 0 = $14 $14 x 150%= **$21.00**

Gustafson, G.	$8.00
Guthrie & Co.; London, England	$14.00
* Haddon; England	$14.00
Hahn, P.H.; NY/Germany	$8.00
Haick, Joseph	$9.00
Hainin, Adam	$8.00
Hale, Bros., John and Samuel	$10.00
Hall, Colley; England	$10.00
Hall, John; England	$10.00
Hall, Johnathan; England	$10.00

Courtesy of Smokey Mountain Knife Works

(a) Brand and Origin Base Value	(b) Handle Material % Value	(c) Artwork % Value	(d) Condition % Value	(e) Collector Value
Haddon England **$14.00**	3-piece Genuine Pearl 14 x 400%= **$56.00**	Blade etching 14 x 300%= **$42.00**	Good **150%**	$56 + $42=$98 $98 x 150%= **$147.00**

Hallam, James; Germany	$10.00
Hallday Bros.; England	$11.00
Halma Shear & Razor Works	$10.00
Halstead, D.C.; England	$10.00
Hambleton, W.B. & Vom Cleff, R.; Philadelphia/England/Germany	$8.00
Hamilton Razor Co.	$11.00
Hammacher Deluis & Co.; NY	$10.00
Hamon Fabricant; Paris, France	$12.00
Hancock, George; England (?)	$9.00
Hancock & Sons; England	$8.00
Hand-Forged Razor Co.; Germany	$11.00
Harder's Gunworks; England	$10.00
Hardy, Thomas; England	$10.00
Hardy, Thomas & Sons; England	$10.00
Hargraves, W. & Sons; England	$11.00
Harlow, Libby & Finn; Boston, MA	$10.00
* Harnack, Moore Co.; St. Louis, MO	$11.00

Courtesy of Smokey Mountain Knife Works

(a) Brand and Origin Base Value	(b) Handle Material % Value	(c) Artwork % Value	(d) Condition % Value	(e) Collector Value
Harnack, Moore Co. St. Louis, MO **$11.00**	Brass Handles 11 x 350%= $38.50 **$39.00**	Floral design high relief 11 x 400%= **$44.00**	Good **150%**	$39 + $44=$83 $83 x 150%= $124.50 **$125.00**

Harper & McIntire Co.; England	$10.00
Harrington Cutlery Co.; MA	$15.00
Harrington, Dexter	$10.00
Harrington, Henry	$12.00
Harrington, Theo; CT	$9.00
Harris Barber Supply; Galesburg, IL	$11.00
Harris J.E. & Son, Warrensburg, MO	$12.00
Harris, C.E.; Brockton, MA	$12.00
Harris-Goar Mfg. Co.; Kansas City, MO	$10.00
Harrison Brothers & Howson; England	$10.00
Harrison, John	$8.00
Harrison, W.	$8.00
Hart, Issac B.; England	$10.00
Hart, Leslie & Warren; England	$9.00
Hart & Nazro; NY	$9.00
Hart & Pitcher; MO	$10.00
Hartford Cutlery Co.; Hartford, CT	$11.00
Hartkoph Cutlery; New York City, NY	$12.00
Harwood, Joseph; England	$10.00
Hassam Bros.; England	$9.00
Hassam, Fred; NY	$8.00
Hassam & Gurley; NY	$9.00
Hastings Cutlery; England	$9.00
Hastings & Gurley; NY	$9.00
Hatch Cutlery; CT	$17.00
Hatem, Nohoum; Germany	$8.00
Hawaiian Barber Supply Co.; HI	$14.00
Hawcroft, R. & Co.; Germany	$9.00
Hawkworth, L.E.; England	$10.00
Hawley Hardware Co.; CT	$11.00
Haydn, R. & Co.; Germany	$10.00
Hayes, M.J.; CA	$10.00
Haywood, J.E.; England	$10.00
Hecker, Charles; OH	$10.00

Heilberg, J.A.; Sweden	$10.00
Heimerdinger, August A.; Louisville, KY	$35.00
Heimerdinger, W.C.; Louisville, KY	$25.00
★ Henckels; Germany	$15.00

Courtesy of Smokey Mountain Knife Works

(a) Brand and Origin Base Value	(b) Handle Material % Value	(c) Artwork % Value	(d) Condition % Value	(e) Collector Value
J.A. Henckels "Twin Works" Germany **$15.00**	Genuine Pearl 15 x 400%= **$60.00**	Carved handles 15 x 400%= **$60.00**	Minor crack, cannont be repaired Collectible- **80%**	$60+$60=$120 $120 x 80%= **$96.00**

Herder, L. & Son; Philadelphia, PA	$11.00
★ Hessenbruch, T. & Co.; Germany	$12.00
Hessenbruch, H. & Co.; Germany	$10.00
★ Hibbard, Spencer & Bartlett; USA	$25.00
Hibbard, R.; England	$10.00
Hibbard, S.; England	$10.00

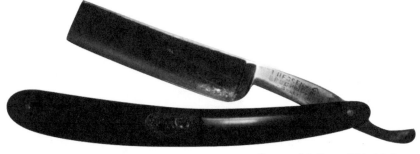

Courtesy of the Dewey Whited Collection

(a) Brand and Origin Base Value	(b) Handle Material % Value	(c) Artwork % Value	(d) Condition % Value	(e) Collector Value
T. Hessenbruch & Co. Germany **$12.00**	Slick Black 12 x 150%= **$18.00**	Imprint stamped in handle 12 x 125%= **$15.00**	Collectible- **80%**	$18 + $15=$33 $33 x 80%= $26.40 **$26.00**

Courtesy of Smokey Mountain Knife Works

(a) Brand and Origin Base Value	(b) Handle Material % Value	(c) Artwork % Value	(d) Condition % Value	(e) Collector Value
Hibbard, Spencer & Bartlett U.S./Germany **$25.00**	Peckbone w/ worm grove 25 x 350%= $87.50 **$88.00**	Blade etch fancy "Heavy Clay" 25 x 200%= **$50.00**	Collectible+ **125%**	$88+$50=$138 $138 x 125%= $172.50 **$173.00**

Higgins, M.J.; England	$10.00
Hilger & Sons; Germany	$10.00
Hill, H.H. & Co.; England	$10.00
Hitchcock-Hill Co.; England	$11.00
Hives; England	$11.00
H.M.C. Cut. Co.; Boston, MA	$18.00
Hobson, H.; England	$9.00
Hobson, H. & Co.; CT/England	$9.00
Hobson, John B.; England	$10.00
Hobson, M.; England	$8.00
Hoffman, E & E; Germany	$10.00
Hoffritz; Germany/NY	$12.00
✶ ✶ Holler, John S. & Co. (Tower Brand)	$14.00
✶ Holley Mfg. Co.; CT	$27.00
Hollinger, J. & Bros.; Fremont, OH	$10.00
Holt, Ed B. & Co.; Boston, MA	$11.00
Holtin, Carl A.; Ridgeway; PA	$11.00
Holtz, Jacob; NY	$8.00
Holtzapffel & Co.; England	$9.00
Holzhaur & Sons; OH	$10.00
Homan & Co.	$8.00
Home Run Razor (Edlis B.S.); Pittsburgh, PA	$10.00
Homer, R.	$7.00

Courtesy of Smokey Mountain Knife Works

(a) Brand and Origin Base Value	(b) Handle Material % Value	(c) Artwork % Value	(d) Condition % Value	(e) Collector Value
J.S. Holler & Co. **$14.00**	3-piece Pearl 14 x 400%= **$56.00**	Silver insert etched blade 14 x 400%= **$56.00**	Good **150%**	$56+$56=$112 $112 x 150%= **$168.00**

Courtesy of Smokey Mountain Knife Works

(a) Brand and Origin Base Value	(b) Handle Material % Value	(c) Artwork % Value	(d) Condition % Value	(e) Collector Value
John S. Holler & Co. "Tower Brand" **$15.00**	3-piece Genuine Pearl 15 x 400%= **$60.00**	Silver bar inlay 15 x 300%= **$45.00**	Good **150%**	$60+$45=$105 $105 x 150%= $157.50 **$158.00**

Courtesy of Smokey Mountain Knife Works

(a) Brand and Origin Base Value	(b) Handle Material % Value	(c) Artwork % Value	(d) Condition % Value	(e) Collector Value
Holly Mfg. Co. Lakeville **$27.00**	Pickbone handles 27 x 350%= $94.50 **$95.00**	Blade etch & bar shield 27 x 200%= **$54.00**	Good **150%**	$95+$54=$149 $149 x 150%= $223.50 **$224.00**

Hon.; France	$11.00
Honey & Skelton; England	$9.00
Hoosier Razor, The (C.G. Grah)	
Indianapolis, IN/Germany	$12.00
* Hope, Albert-Schmidt Co.; Germany	$12.00

Courtesy of Smokey Mountain Knife Works

(a) Brand and Origin Base Value	(b) Handle Material % Value	(c) Artwork % Value	(d) Condition % Value	(e) Collector Value
Hope Cutlery Albert-Schmidt Germany **$12.00**	Slick Black 12 x 150%= **$18.00**	Standing nude w/ grape clusters 12 x 300%= **$36.00**	Good **150%**	$18+ $36=$54 $54 x 150%= **$81.00**

Horace, J.	$8.00
Horn, W.C., Bros. & Co.; Germany	$8.00
Hornet; Germany	$10.00
Horrabins; England	$9.00
Horstense Razor Co.	$8.00
Horster, Gmbh & Co.	$9.00
Horton & Co.	$9.00
Houghton & Co.	$9.00
Hovender, R. & Sons; England	$11.00
Hovland, S.	$8.00
Howard Razor Co.; MA	$10.00
Howard-Lux Co.; OH	$10.00
Howe, Original; Germany	$10.00
Howell & Co.	$10.00
Hudson, John	$8.00
Hummel, Kurt	$7.00
Humphrey's; England	$9.00
Hunold, Ernest; Providence, RI/England	$11.00

Hunt, Johnathan; England	$10.00
Hunts, A.	$8.00
Hunter; England	$8.00
Hunter & Son; England	$10.00
Huntington Barber Supply Co.; Huntington, WV	$10.00
Hustler; Germany	$9.00
Hutchenson, W & H; England	$9.00
I.A.K.; Germany	$9.00
Ibbotson, Peace & Co.; England	$14.00
I.H.S., Rose; USA/England	$10.00
Ilium Barber Supply Co.; NY	$10.00
Ill-Mo Supply Co.; St. Louis, MO	$11.00
Illinois Razor Supply & Cutlery Corp.; Chicago, IL	$12.00
* Imperial Razor Co.; Germany	$12.00

Courtesy of the Dewey Whited Collection

(a) Brand and Origin Base Value	(b) Handle Material % Value	(c) Artwork % Value	(d) Condition % Value	(e) Collector Value
Imperial Razor Co. Germany **$12.00**	Black Horn 12 x 150%= **$18.00**	Interesting blade etch 12 x 200%= **$24.00**	Collectible **100%**	$18 + $24=$42 $42 x 100%= **$42.00**

International Corp.; Germany	$11.00
* International Cutlery Co.; New York, NY/Germany	$8.00
International Shear Co.; PA	$12.00
I & S; USA	$9.00
I.W.S.; England	$9.00
I.X.L.; England	$14.00
Jack Knife Ben; Chicago, IL	$17.00

Courtesy of Smokey Mountain Knife Works

(a) Brand and Origin Base Value	(b) Handle Material % Value	(c) Artwork % Value	(d) Condition % Value	(e) Collector Value
International Cutlery Co. NY, NY/ Germany **$8.00**	"Cracked Ice" Celluloid handles 8 x 300%= **$24.00**	Very fancy logo & brand inlay 8 x 200%= **$16.00**	Collectible **100%**	$24 + $16=$40 $40 x 100%= **$40.00**

Jackson; Freemont, OH	$16.00
Jackson, Charles; OH	$11.00
Jackson Knife & Shear (J.K.S.); OH	$16.00
Jackson, William & Co.; England	$11.00
Jackson & Sons, Sheath Island Works; England	$10.00
Jacoby & Wester (Wester Bros.); NY	$10.00
Jaeger Barber Supply Co.; MO	$11.00
Jaeger, Joe; Los Angeles, CA	$12.00
Jahn, E.J. & Co.; Detroit	$10.00
James, J.V. & Son; NY	$9.00
Jansen, Emil; Germany	$9.00
Jansen, W.H.; Germany	$9.00
Jassiano & Co.; Germany	$9.00
Jassikno, Faliel D.; Germany	$9.00
Jay, John; NY	$10.00
Jeeb, N.A. Mollub & Co.	$8.00
Jenner, Newstub; St. James St., England	$10.00
Jermanise Cutlery Works	$10.00
Jetter & Scheereer; Germany	$9.00
Jewett & Butler	$9.00
J.H.M.; England	$9.00
Joan's Mfg. Co.; IL	$10.00
Johansen & Peterson; Chicago	$10.00

John, Feli	$9.00
Johnas & Colver (I & C); England	$10.00
Johnson B & B Co.; Montgomery, AL	$16.00
Johnson & Co.; England	$10.00
Johnson, G.; Germany	$10.00
Johnson, James; IL	$10.00
Johnson, J.C.; Rockford, IL	$11.00
Johnson, J.T.; Germany	$9.00
Johnson Mfg Co.; England	$10.00
Johnson Silver Steel Razor	$10.00
Johnson Western Works	$14.00
Johnson, William	$12.00
Johnson & Williams; Poughkeepsie, NY	$12.00
Jones & Son; Germany	$8.00
Jones Mfg Co.; Chicago, IL	$10.00
Joppa, J. Brommall Mark	$10.00
Jordan, Albert & Co.; NY	$12.00
Jordeau, Jean Inc.; NY	$10.00
Jordon, A.J.; England/Germany/St. Louis	$10.00
Jordon, Andrew & Co.; England/Germany/St. Louis	$10.00
Joseph, Nathan & Co.; San Francisco, CA	$12.00
Joseph, S.	$9.00
J.R. & Sons	$9.00
Jung, M.; NY/Germany	$7.00
Jureidini, Nasib; England	$9.00
Jureidini, Said Khalil; NY	$11.00
Justice, A.R., Co.; England/Philadelphia	$10.00
Justice, Paris	$10.00
* KaBar, Union Cut. Co.; USA	$28.00
Kahnweiler, S.B., & Co.; NY	$9.00
Kain-Abel; Germany	$10.00
Kaiser, Gustov; Germany	$12.00
Kaldenberg, F.J.	$10.00
Kalsted, D.C.; England	$10.00

Courtesy of the Dewey Whited Collection

(a) Brand and Origin Base Value	(b) Handle Material % Value	(c) Artwork % Value	(d) Condition % Value	(e) Collector Value
KaBar USA **$28.00**	Hard Rubber 28 x 150%= **$42.00**	Interesting blade design — model # on handle 28 x 125%= **$35.00**	Collectible **100%**	$42+ $35= $77 $77 x 100%= **$77.00**

Kama; Germany	$8.00
Kane, Masu; Germany	$10.00
★ Kanner, J.; Solingen, Germany	$6.00
Karayoz, Cifte; Germany	$8.00
Karim, Bazil; Spain	$11.00
Karnak More Co.; USA	$8.00
Kastor, Adolf; Germany	$9.00
Kastor Bros.; Germany	$10.00

Courtesy of Smokey Mountain Knife Works

(a) Brand and Origin Base Value	(b) Handle Material % Value	(c) Artwork % Value	(d) Condition % Value	(e) Collector Value
J. Kanner Solingen, Germany **$6.00**	Ivory Celluloid 6 x 300%= **$18.00**	Etched blade fancy bolsters 6 x 200%= **$12.00**	Collectible **100%**	$18 + $12=$30 $30 x 100%= **$30.00**

Kattell, Stanley M.; Binghampton, NY	$14.00
Keeler, F.M. Co.; Boston, MA	$11.00
* Keen Kutter; USA	$16.00
* Keene Cut. Co.; Germany	$14.00
Keidel, Henry & Co.; Germany	$10.00
Keller, Edward A.; Boston, MA	$14.00
Kelly, Howe, Thomson Co.; Duluth, MN	$12.00
Kelly Hardware Co.; USA	$10.00
Kelly, Robert; England	$9.00
Kennedy, Bradford & Sons & MeGuive; USA	$14.00
Kern, R & W; Canada/England	$9.00

Courtesy of the Dewey Whited Collection

(a) Brand and Origin Base Value	(b) Handle Material % Value	(c) Artwork % Value	(d) Condition % Value	(e) Collector Value
Keen Kutter USA **$16.00**	Slick Black 16 x 150%= **$24.00**	Handle inlay gold blade etch 16 x 350%= **$56.00**	Collectible- Broken handle **50%**	$24 + $56=$80 $80 x 50%= **$40.00**

Courtesy of Smokey Mountain Knife Works

(a) Brand and Origin Base Value	(b) Handle Material % Value	(c) Artwork % Value	(d) Condition % Value	(e) Collector Value
Keene Cutlery Co. Germany **$14.00**	Pick Bone 14 x 350%= **$49.00**	Blade etch 14 x 200%= **$28.00**	Good **150%**	$49 + $28=$77 $77 x 150%= $115.50 **$116.00**

Kieblitz; Germany	$11.00
★ Kinfolks Inc.; Little Valley, NY	$28.00
King, M. & J.; NY	$13.00
King Razor Mfg. Co.; PA	$10.00
Kingman & Hassam; Boston, MA	$11.00
Kirby, S.; Germany	$8.00
Kirchmer Supply Co.; LA, CA	$10.00
Kirkham & Co.; England	$10.00
Kirscher, J. & Sohne; CA	$10.00
Klaas, Karl; Germany	$12.00
Klass, Robert; NY/Germany	$12.00
Klass, (Crane Brand); Germany	$14.00
Klauberg, Daniel; NY	$10.00
Klauberg & Sons; NY	$10.00
Kleiblatt Barber Supply, Inc.; Sioux City, IA	$12.00
Kleineick, Ed; Germany	$10.00
Klouberg & Bros.; NY/Germany	$10.00
Kiecht Mfg. Co.; Chicago, IL	$12.00
Knicht, D&F; OH	$11.00
Knetch, G; Germany	$10.00
Knotte, C.F.; Germany	$10.00
Knouth, Gusdtav; Germany	$10.00

Courtesy of the Dewey Whited Collection

(a) Brand and Origin Base Value	(b) Handle Material % Value	(c) Artwork % Value	(d) Condition % Value	(e) Collector Value
Kinfolks Inc. Little Valley, NY **$28.00**	Genuine Ivory 28 x 550%= **$154.00**	Plain 28 x 100%= **$28.00**	Collectible- **90%**	$154 + $28 = $182 $182 x 90%= $163.80 **$164.00**

87

Kobar; Germany	$10.00
Kobesco; Germany	$9.00
Koch, F.A. & Co; Germany/NY	$10.00
Koch, J.; IL	$11.00
Koch, Theo; Chicago, IL	$11.00
Koch, Shafer; Germany	$10.00
Koeller, Oligs Co.; Germany	$10.00
Koeller & Smitz Co.; Germany	$9.00
Koelsch & Shoffer; Germany	$9.00
Koercher, J.B.; Germany	$9.00
Koken Barber Supply; Germany	$9.00
Koken; St. Louis, MO	$11.00
Koller, H.; Germany	$10.00
Konejung; Germany	$10.00
Korhammer, C.	$9.00
* Korn Razor Mfg. Co.; Little Valley, NY	$20.00
Korte, G.; Germany	$10.00
Kovalt & Smith; PA	$14.00
Kramerso; Germany	$7.00
Krank, Alfred; St. Paul, MN	$10.00
Krant, E.; OH	$9.00

Courtesy of the Dewey Whited Collection

(a) Brand and Origin Base Value	(b) Handle Material % Value	(c) Artwork % Value	(d) Condition % Value	(e) Collector Value
Korn Razor Mfg. Co. Little Valley, NY **$20.00**	Clear Amber Colored Plastic 20 x 125%= **$25.00**	Nonexistent **0**	Collectible- **80%**	$25 + 0 = $25 $25 x 80%= **$20.00**

Kraut & Dahna; Chicago/Germany	$7.00
Krohner, Fred; Germany	$10.00
Kron, E.; Germany	$9.00
Kroner Hdw. Co.; Germany	$9.00
Kropp; Germany	$10.00
Krupp; England	$11.00
Kruse & Bahlmann Hdw.; Cincinnati, OH	$15.00
* Krusius Bros.; Germany	$8.00

Courtesy of Smokey Mountain Knife Works

(a) Brand and Origin Base Value	(b) Handle Material % Value	(c) Artwork % Value	(d) Condition % Value	(e) Collector Value
Krusius Bros. Germany **$8.00**	Ivory Celluloid 8 x 300%= **$24.00**	Standing nude & flora 8 x 500%= **$40.00**	Good **150%**	$24 + $40=$64 $64 x 150%= **$96.00**

Kunde, S. & Sonn; Germany	$9.00
Kut-Well; USA	$16.00
L & A Co.; USA	$11.00
LaComte, Renold; France	$12.00
LaCross	$10.00
Lafayette Cut. Co.; Germany	$12.00
* Lakeside Cut. Co.; Chicago, IL	$20.00
Lamb; OH	$10.00
Lambert, E.C.; Flint, MI	$14.00
Lambert & White; MI	$12.00
Lamerse, O.S.; TX	$12.00
Landers, Fraley & Clark; CT, USA	$30.00
* Landsman, A.; New York/Germany	$11.00
Lang, Gebt.; OH	$9.00
Langbein, C.; England	$9.00

Courtesy of Smokey Mountain Knife Works

(a) Brand and Origin Base Value	(b) Handle Material % Value	(c) Artwork % Value	(d) Condition % Value	(e) Collector Value
Lakeside Cutlery Co. Chicago, IL **$20.00**	Brown & Cream Color Composition 20 x 100%= **$20.00**	Fancy bolsters and blade etch soldiers & slogan 20 x 200%= **$40.00**	Collectible **100%**	$20 + $40=$60 $60 x 100%= **$60.00**

Courtesy of Smokey Mountain Knife Works

(a) Brand and Origin Base Value	(b) Handle Material % Value	(c) Artwork % Value	(d) Condition % Value	(e) Collector Value
A. Landsman NY/Germany **$11.00**	Genuine Ivory 11 x 550%= $60.50 **$61.00**	Scrimshaw of sea monster & sailing ship 11 x 450%= $49.50 **$50.00**	Good **150%**	$61+$50=$111 $111 x 150%= $166.50 **$167.00**

Larissa; England	$9.00
Larkin; England	$11.00
LaSalle Cut. Co.; IL	$15.00
Law, Ch.; England	$11.00
Law, John; England	$9.00
Lawman & Carey; Independence, MO	$10.00
Lawrence Pub. Co.; Germany	$8.00
* Lawton Cut. Co.; Chicago	$9.00
L.B. Ltd.; Canada	$20.00
L.B. Ltd; England	$9.00

Courtesy of Smokey Mountain Knife Works

(a) Brand and Origin Base Value	(b) Handle Material % Value	(c) Artwork % Value	(d) Condition % Value	(e) Collector Value
The Lawton Cutlery Co. Chicago **$9.00**	Celluloid 9 x 300%= **$27.00**	Ear of corn design 9 x 350%= $31.50 **$32.00**	Good **150%**	$27 + $32=$59 $59 x 150%= $88.50 **$89.00**

L.C.A. Hdw Co.	$10.00
Leader; England	$9.00
LeChampion; Switzerland	$10.00
LeCocltre, Jacque; Switzerland	$12.00
Le Grelot	$10.00
Lee Mfg.; Chicago, IL	$17.00
Lee's Radium Co. Ltd.; England	$10.00
Lehod Yazbek; OH	$10.00
Lehrkind & Paevel Co.; Germany	$9.00
Lehuer; Germany	$9.00
Leineke, J.C.; IN	$10.00
Lenox Cut. Co.; Germany	$11.00
Leon, A.; England	$10.00
Leopold, R.; Germany	$8.00
Lerner; England	$10.00
* Le Royal, Tranchant & Crown; France	$10.00
Levenson, L.; Louisville, KY	$15.00
* Levering Razor Co.; NY/Germany	$18.00
Lewgold Imp. Co.; NY	$10.00
Lewis Brothers & Co. "Klean Kutter"; Montreal, Canada	$10.00
Lewis Razor Co.; Germany	$10.00
Leyet A Tours; France	$11.00

Courtesy of Smokey Mountain Knife Works

(a) Brand and Origin Base Value	(b) Handle Material % Value	(c) Artwork % Value	(d) Condition % Value	(e) Collector Value
Le Royal Tranchant & Crown "DeLafoul Mouse" France **$10.00**	Slick Black 10 x 150%= **$15.00**	Blade worked brass & genuine pearl inlay 10 x 300%= **$30.00**	Collectible **100%**	$15 + $30=$45 $45 x 100%= **$45.00**

Courtesy of Smokey Mountain Knife Works

(a) Brand and Origin Base Value	(b) Handle Material % Value	(c) Artwork % Value	(d) Condition % Value	(e) Collector Value
Levering Razor Co. NY/Germany **$18.00**	Ivory Celluloid 18 x 300%= **$54.00**	Standing nude & floral design 18 x 500%= **$90.00**	Pin Replaced Collectible- 75%	$54 + 90=$144 $144 x 75%= **$108.00**

L.F. & C.; CT, USA	$30.00
L.G. & Co.; Germany	$9.00
Liberty Cut. Co.; Germany	$12.00
Libby, Harlow & Co.; MA	$10.00
Life, Warburtion's Narj; England	$9.00
Liggetts; NY	$7.00
Limerick, "Hall's Mark"; England	$10.00
Linden; England	$10.00
Lindsay, Mfg. Co., H; Pittsburgh, PA	$11.00
Lindsay, J. Hwd. Co.; Pittsburgh, PA	$11.00
Lindsay Co Serritt; Phil., PA	$11.00
Linguard, John; England	$9.00

Linton & Pass Mfg. Co.; PA	$10.00
Lion Razor Works; Germany	$12.00
Litt, George; Germany	$10.00
Little & Co., Charles; Germany	$11.00
Little Valley Knife Co.; NY	$35.00+
Lockword Bros.; England	$12.00
Lodis	$9.00
* Loeffler Co.; Rochester, NY	$10.00
Loew, Wm.; Des Moines, IA	$12.00
Logan-Greg Hwd. Co.; Louisville, KY	$8.00
London Razor Co.; Germany	$12.00
Long & Co., H.G.; England	$9.00
Lord & Harvey; England	$11.00
Loreno, W.F.	$9.00
Louper; Germany	$9.00
Lowe Co.; WI, USA	$10.00
L.S. Co.; England	$8.00
L.S. & N.; Leoder, Germany	$9.00
Ludo Shear & Razor Works; Germany	$10.00
Lund; Germany	$10.00
Lutters, Karl; Germany	$9.00

Courtesy of the Dewey Whited Collection

(a) Brand and Origin Base Value	(b) Handle Material % Value	(c) Artwork % Value	(d) Condition % Value	(e) Collector Value
Loeffler Co. Rochester, NY **$10.00**	Celluloid (colorful) 10 x 300%= **$30.00**	Plain 10 x 100%= **$10.00**	Collectible **100%**	$30 + $10=$40 $40 x 100%= **$40.00**

Lyre & Co.; England	$11.00
M's Co.; PA	$10.00
MAB Reg.; Germany	$9.00
MacDaniel; London, England	$10.00
MacKenzie; Edinburgh, Scotland	$13.00
Macomber, Bigelow, & Dowse; Boston, MA	$10.00
Madison, L.J. Co.; OH	$11.00
Madler, Julius & Sohn; Germany	$10.00
Magdeburg, H.G.; NY	$11.00
Magic (Eagle Pencil Co.); NY	$11.00
Magnetic Cutlery Co.; Germany	$10.00
Maher & Grosh; OH	$25.00
Mahfoud & O'Toole	$9.00
* Maine Barber Supply Co.; Portland, ME	$10.00
Makham & Son; Germany	$10.00
Makrauer Barber Supply; PA	$12.00
Malliburton; Germany	$10.00
Mallin, E.; England	$11.00
Mallinson; England	$10.00
Malluk, Nejeeb; Germany	$9.00
Maly, K.; Germany	$8.00
Manchester Razor Co.; Germany	$11.00
Mangoon, E.; England	$10.00

Courtesy of Smokey Mountain Knife Works

(a) Brand and Origin Base Value	(b) Handle Material % Value	(c) Artwork % Value	(d) Condition % Value	(e) Collector Value
Maine B.S. Co. Portland, ME **$10.00**	Waterfall Celluloid Handles 10 x 300%= **$30.00**	Antique car inlay 10 x 200%= **$20.00**	Good **150%**	$30 + $20=$50 $50 x 150%= **$75.00**

Manhattan Cutlery Co.; England	$15.00
Mann & Co.; OH	$7.00
Mansour, T. & Sons; NY	$10.00
Many, George & Co.; England	$10.00
Mappin, Joseph; England	$10.00
Mappin Bros.; England	$9.00
Mappin & Webb Ltd.; England	$12.00
Markos & Bros.; Germany	$9.00
Marmar, W. & Co.; England	$9.00
Marples & Co.; England	$10.00
Marriot, Luke; England	$10.00
Marsden; England	$11.00
Marsh, John; England	$9.00
Marsh Bros. & Co.; England	$12.00
Marshall Wells Hdw.; NY	$11.00
Marshes & Shephard; England	$12.00
Martin & Gannaway Bailey's Choice; VA	$14.00
Martin; Germany	$8.00
Marvy Co., Wm.; MN	$11.00
Maryland Barber Sup.; MD	$10.00
Mason; USA	$7.00
Matheisen, M.; Germany	$8.00
Mathews & Lively; Atlanta/Germany	$11.00
Mawson, S. & Sons, Shef	$10.00
May & Thomas Hdw. Co.; AL	$14.00
MayBee Razor Co.; USA	$20.00
Mayer, G.M.; NY	$10.00
McClory, J.E.; England	$10.00
McClung, C.M. & Co.; Knoxville, TN	$10.00
McCoy & Co., KY	$10.00
McDonald, W.E.; MA	$11.00
McGill Cutlery Co.; CA	$10.00
McIntosh & Heather; OH	$12.00
McKeever Bros.; IA	$14.00

McKenna; Geneva, NY	$10.00
McKenzie; Edinburgh, Scotland	$13.00
McLaughlins; USA	$7.00
Mclean Black & Co.; MO	$10.00
Mcland; Belfast, Ireland	$10.00
McIlwaine, N. & H.; USA	$9.00
McMoran, J. & Co.; MA	$10.00
McNamera; Boston, MA	$11.00
McQueen Sup. Co.; KY	$12.00
Mehl & Sapper; PA	$8.00
* Meier; Germany	$10.00

Courtesy of Smokey Mountain Knife Works

(a) Brand and Origin Base Value	(b) Handle Material % Value	(c) Artwork % Value	(d) Condition % Value	(e) Collector Value
Meier Germany **$10.00**	Black & Gold Mottled Celluloid 10 x 300%= **$30.00**	Abalone insert fancy blade etch 10 x 300%= **$30.00**	Collectible+ **125%**	$30 + $30=$60 $60 x 125%= **$75.00**

Meifer, J.; England	$11.00
Melchior, Hugo; Omaha/Germany	$8.00
Melchior, Bro.; Chicago, USA	$11.00
Mellhuise & Hoborn; Germany	$9.00
Menthoote; England	$11.00
Meredith, J.L.; MA	$10.00
Merit Import Co.; Germany	$7.00
Messerschmidth; Pakistan	$7.00
Metropolitan Cutlery Co.; NY	$12.00
* M & H Grinding Co.; Cleveland, OH/NY	$10.00
Michaels, Peter; NY	$16.00
Microscopic; Germany	$9.00

* Middlebrooks, B.W. Co.; Georgia	$14.00
Middleton Cutlery Co.; England	$10.00
Middleton, John; England	$10.00
Migone & Co.; CA	$10.00
Milin, A.; England	$8.00
Miller & Sons (Blue Steel); OH	$11.00
Milner, M.; USA	$9.00
Milwaukee Barber Supply; WI	$10.00
Mithoff, H.; OH	$9.00
Mizzoo Cut. Co.; St. Louis, MO	$12.00
Mobson	$9.00
Model Barber Supply; Peoria, IL	$12.00

Courtesy of Smokey Mountain Knife Works

(a) Brand and Origin Base Value	(b) Handle Material % Value	(c) Artwork % Value	(d) Condition % Value	(e) Collector Value
M & H Grinding Co Cleveland, OH **$10.00**	Ivory Celluloid 10 x 300%= **$30.00**	Floral motif inlay 10 x 400%= **$40.00**	Collectible **100%**	$30 + $40=$70 $70 x 100%= **$70.00**

Courtesy of the Dewey Whited Collection

(a) Brand and Origin Base Value	(b) Handle Material % Value	(c) Artwork % Value	(d) Condition % Value	(e) Collector Value
B.W. Middlebrooks Georgia **$14.00**	Hard Rubber 14 x 150%= **$21.00**	Nonexistent **0**	Collectible+ **125%**	$21 + 0=$21 $21 x 125%= $26.25 **$26.00**

Mogel, M. Inc.; NY	$10.00
Mohawk Valley Barber Supply Co.; NY	$13.00
Mokoto; Germany	$6.00
* Moler System of Colleges; Germany	$14.00

Courtesy of Smokey Mountain Knife Works

(a) Brand and Origin Base Value	(b) Handle Material % Value	(c) Artwork % Value	(d) Condition % Value	(e) Collector Value
Moler System of Colleges Germany **$14.00**	3-piece Pearl 14 x 400%= **$56.00**	Dated 1895 gunstock handles 14 x 300%= **$42.00**	Good **150%**	$56 + $42=$98 $98 x 150%= **$147.00**

Money Bak Razor Co.; NY	$12.00
Monkhouse, Carl; NY	$10.00
Monroe Cutlery; NY	$14.00
Monserrat, Jesse; France	$10.00
Monumental Cutlery Co.; England	$12.00
Moore Co.; MO	$8.00
Moore & Handley Hardware; AL	$10.00
Moore, K.; MO	$8.00
Moran, J.M & Co.	$10.00
Morehouse & Wells; IL	$11.00
Morgan, T.; USA	$10.00
Morlaix, M.	$8.00
Morley W.H. & Co.; Austria	$11.00
Morris Mfg. Co.; MI	$10.00
Morrison Co.	$8.00
Morton, J.; Oxford, England	$11.00
Moshy & Rabaim; Canada	$10.00
Mosley & Sons; England	$11.00
Mount, J.T. & Co.; England	$10.00

M.S. & W. Co.; NY	$10.00
Mulenoto Werke; Germany	$9.00
Muller, C.	$10.00
Muskegan Barber Supply Co.; MI	$9.00
* * Najeeb Molluk Co.; Japan	$11.00
Nance & Sons; Wichita, KS	$10.00
Nantz, H.	$8.00
Nash Hardware Co.; Ft. Worth, TX	$11.00

Courtesy of the Dewey Whited Collection

(a) Brand and Origin Base Value	(b) Handle Material % Value	(c) Artwork % Value	(d) Condition % Value	(e) Collector Value
Najeeb Molluk Co. Japan **$11.00**	Bakelite 11 x 150%= $16.50 **$17.00**	Ornate blade etching 11 x 200%= **$22.00**	Collectible+ **125%**	$17 + $22=$39 $39 x 125%= $48.75 **$49.00**

Courtesy of Smokey Mountain Knife Works

(a) Brand and Origin Base Value	(b) Handle Material % Value	(c) Artwork % Value	(d) Condition % Value	(e) Collector Value
Najeeb Molluk Co. Japan **$11.00**	Red & Yellow Celluloid 11 x 300%= **$33.00**	Scroll work handles blade etch NY Harbor sailing ship 11 x 550%= $60.50 **$61.00**	Good **150%**	$33 + $61=$94 $94 x 150%= **$141.00**

National Barber Supply; GA	$10.00
National Cut. Co.; OH	$11.00
National Mfg. Co.; GA	$10.00
Naylor & Sanderson; England	$8.00
Needham Bros.; England	$8.00
Needham, Veal & Tyzack; England	$10.00
Neilson, N. Co.; NY	$10.00
Nelson Razor Co.; ME	$9.00
Neumeyer & Diamond; NY	$11.00
Neva-Hone Razor Co.; NY	$14.00
Never Dull Cutlery Co.; USA	$12.00
New Century Cutlery Co.; Germany	$9.00
New England Cutlery Co.; USA	$16.00
New England Razor Co.; Boston	$18.00
New York Knife Co.; USA	$22.00
New York Razor Co.; USA	$18.00
Newhause, Fredrick; Germany	$8.00
Newton, Francis; England	$8.00
Niagara Cut. Co.; Germany	$10.00
Nicholson, I.; England	$10.00
Nicholson & Son; England	$10.00
Nicholson, W.M.; England	$10.00
Nicholson & Co.; England	$10.00
Nixon & Co.; England	$8.00
Nobson, Francis	$8.00
Noell, Wilhelm; Germany	$10.00
Non-Felt Razor Works; MO/Germany	$10.00
* Non-Plus; Germany	$18.00
* Noonan, T. & Sons; Boston, MA	$10.00
Nordfelt, Guistaf; Germany	$10.00
Norris, Samuel; England	$10.00
Norleigh; England	$8.00
Northern; NY	$10.00
Northfield Cut. Co.; CT	$18.00

Courtesy of Smokey Mountain Knife Works

(a) Brand and Origin Base Value	(b) Handle Material % Value	(c) Artwork % Value	(d) Condition % Value	(e) Collector Value
Non-Plus Ultra "Crown & Sword" Germany **$18.00**	Genuine Stag 18 x 400%= **$72.00**	Bar shield 18 x 100%= **$18.00**	Good **150%**	$72 + $18=$90 $90 x 150%= **$135.00**

Courtesy of Smokey Mountain Knife Works

(a) Brand and Origin Base Value	(b) Handle Material % Value	(c) Artwork % Value	(d) Condition % Value	(e) Collector Value
T. Noonan & Sons Boston, MA **$10.00**	Green Celluloid 10 x 300%= **$30.00**	Inlaid w/ words "Minute Man," image of person & U.S. flag 10 x 300%= **$30.00**	Collectible **100%**	$30 + $30=$60 $60 x 100%= **$60.00**

Norvelle-Shapleigh; St. Louis	$20.00
Norwich Cut. Co.; USA	$12.00
Novelty Cut. Co.; USA	$18.00
Nowell, J.; England	$9.00
Nowill & Sons; England	$12.00
Nowill & Kippax; England	$10.00
Oak Razor Works; England	$10.00
Oberhauser, Martin; Germany	$9.00

O.C. Barber Supply Co.; OH	$12.00
O'Donnel, J.A.	$10.00
Ohio Farmer; OH	$16.00
Old Forge; NY	$20.00
Olean Cut. Co.; NY	$22.00
Omega; Germany	$8.00
Onondago Barber Supply House; NY	$11.00
* Ontario Cut. Co.; Geneva, NY	$18.00

Courtesy of the Dewey Whited Collection

(a) Brand and Origin Base Value	(b) Handle Material % Value	(c) Artwork % Value	(d) Condition % Value	(e) Collector Value
Ontario Cut. Co. Geneva, NY **$18.00**	Celluloid 18 x 300%= **$54.00**	Attractive 18 x 100%= **$18.00**	Good **150%**	$54 + $18=$72 $72 x 150%= **$108.00**

Ophir No. 2; Germany	$10.00
Orosdam, A.; England	$10.00
Osborne & Co.; USA	$12.00
Osgood, Bray & Co.; CA/Germany	$10.00
Owl Brand; England	$7.00
* Oxford Razor Co.; Germany	$10.00
Oxley, Isaac; England	$9.00
Pabst & Kohler; OH	$12.00
Packard Hardware Co.; PA	$10.00
Packwood; England	$7.00
Painton, George; NY	$8.00
Pairo Barber Supply; MO	$10.00
Pal-Lin Mfg. Co.; IN	$11.00
Palfreyman, George; England	$10.00

Courtesy of Smokey Mountain Knife Works

(a) Brand and Origin Base Value	(b) Handle Material % Value	(c) Artwork % Value	(d) Condition % Value	(e) Collector Value
Oxford Razor Co. Germany **$10.00**	Ivory Celluloid 10 x 300%= **$30.00**	Handpainted eagle & flags 10 x 350%= **$35.00**	Collectible **100%**	$30 + $35=$65 $65 x 100%= **$65.00**

Palmer; Chicago, IL	$15.00
Palmer & Bachelder; OH	$15.00
* Palmer Brothers; Savannah, GA	$20.00

Courtesy of Smokey Mountain Knife Works

(a) Brand and Origin Base Value	(b) Handle Material % Value	(c) Artwork % Value	(d) Condition % Value	(e) Collector Value
Palmer Brothers Savannah, GA **$20.00**	Genuine Ivory 20 x 550%= **$110.00**	Blade hand forged 20 x 150%= **$30.00**	Collectible+ **125%**	$110 + $30 = $140 $140 x 125%= **$175.00**

Panama Supply Co.; Germany	$10.00
Pan American Razor Co.; USA	$12.00
Pan Handle Barber Supply Co.; WV	$11.00
Panderborn, Gebr.; Germany	$8.00
Parke	$7.00
Parker Barber Supply; TX	$9.00
Parker Chemical Co.; IN	$9.00
Parker, Josephus; USA	$7.00
Parker, G.A.; PA	$10.00
Parker, Widow	$9.00

Parker & Linley; England	$10.00
Parkins; England	$7.00
Parramore, S.; England	$8.00
Patent Tempered	$8.00
Patten, Hannah & Son	$9.00
Pauls Brothers (E. Weck); NY	$10.00
Payne & Sons; NY	$12.00
Pearce, Henry; England	$9.00
Pearce, I.; England	$11.00
Pearl Duck; Germany	$12.00
Pearson; England	$10.00
Peerless Cut. Co.; NY	$18.00
Pennsylvania Preferred Barber Supply Co.; PA	$10.00
Peoria Barber Supply; IL	$11.00
Peres, D.; Germany	$8.00
∗ Pergrin Hardware Co.; Columbus, OH	$10.00

Courtesy of Smokey Mountain Knife Works

(a) Brand and Origin Base Value	(b) Handle Material % Value	(c) Artwork % Value	(d) Condition % Value	(e) Collector Value
Pergrin Hardware Co. Columbus, OH **$10.00**	Colorful Cellu- loid Handles 10 x 300%= **$30.00**	3 bells etched on blade 10 x 200%= **$20.00**	Collectible **100%**	$30 + $20=$50 $50 x 100%= **$50.00**

Perlmann, L.; Leipzig, Germany	$9.00
Perry Barber Supply	$9.00
Peter, Stan & Warren Schaft; Germany	$10.00
Petty, John & Sons; England	$11.00
Peukert, J.; Germany	$9.00
Philadelphia Barber Supply; PA	$15.00
Phillips; NJ	$10.00
Phoenix Cut. Co.; NY	$14.00

Picard; France	$12.00
Pick, Slayer & Co.; England	$10.00
Pickering Hdw. & Cut. Co.; OH	$11.00
Pieper; OH/Germany	$9.00
Pike Mfg. Co.; NH	$13.00
Pioneer Barber Supply Co.; IL	$11.00
Pippin, Theo; England	$10.00
Pitts, J.; England	$11.00
Plato, W.P.; IL	$10.00
Platts, C. & Sons; PA	$16.00
Plum, George; England	$9.00
Plumacher	$12.00
Plunkett, L.; Germany	$10.00
Post Shear Co.; MA	$11.00
Potter, J.H.; England	$10.00
Premco; Germany	$8.00
Premier Cut Co.; Germany	$10.00
* Price M.; San Francisco, CA	$75.00

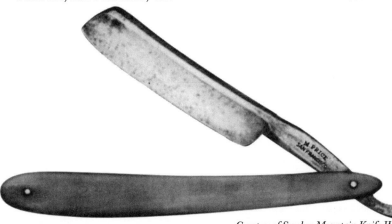

Courtesy of Smokey Mountain Knife Works

(a) Brand and Origin Base Value	(b) Handle Material % Value	(c) Artwork % Value	(d) Condition % Value	(e) Collector Value
M. Price San Francisco, CA **$75.00**	Genuine Ivory 75 x 550%= $412.50 **$413.00**	Nonexistent **0**	Good for its age (150 yrs.) **150%**	$413 + 0=$413 $413 x 150%= $619.50 **$620.00**

Listings of Companies & Base Values

Pride of Solingen; Germany	$9.00
Prima; Germany	$9.00
Primble, John (Belknap); Louisville, KY	$22.00
* Primble, John E., India Steel Works; Louisville, KY	$22.00

Courtesy of Smokey Mountain Knife Works

(a) Brand and Origin Base Value	(b) Handle Material % Value	(c) Artwork % Value	(d) Condition % Value	(e) Collector Value
John Primble India Steel Works Louisville, KY **$22.00**	Peach Seed Bone 22 x 350%= **$77.00**	Blade etch "Southern Gentleman," bar shield 22 x 200%= **$44.00**	Good **150%**	$77+$44=$121 $121 x 150%= $181.50 **$182.00**

Primble, John (Belknap); Louisville, KY/Germany	$20.00
Primble, John, Belknap Hdw. & Mfg. Co.; Louisville, KY	$20.00
Prince; John; Germany	$10.00
Princeton Barber Supply Co.; IN	$11.00
Pritzlaff Hardware Co.; WI	$10.00
Proebsting & Co.; USA	$9.00
Progress 665; Germany	$9.00
Providence; England	$11.00
Pryof, Michael; England	$10.00
Puma; Germany	$18.00
Pumecker, G.H.; NY/Germany	$9.00
Punjo; Germany	$8.00
Pure, Simon Cutlery Co.; Germany	$13.00

Purr Co.; England	$9.00
Pursley & Hitch Barber Supply; OH	$9.00
Pyl, J.; OH	$8.00
Quaker City Cutlery Co.; PA	$12.00
Qualite Superiurf	$10.00
Queen City; NY	$30.00
Querelle, A.; Paris, France	$12.00
Quigley; Germany	$8.00
Quinby & Son; Germany	$9.00
Radford, Joseph & Sons; England	$11.00
Radimite Co.; Chicago, IL	$10.00
Rafla Hardware	$10.00
Ragg, John & William; England	$12.00
* Rahim & Malil; Germany	$10.00

Courtesy of Smokey Mountain Knife Works

(a) Brand and Origin Base Value	(b) Handle Material % Value	(c) Artwork % Value	(d) Condition % Value	(e) Collector Value
Rahim & Malil Germany **$10.00**	Red & Yellow Stripe Celluloid 10 x 300%= **$30.00**	Attractive handles 10 x 200%= **$20.00**	Collectible+ **125%**	$30 + $20=$50 $50 x 125%= $62.50 **$63.00**

Ramapo Co.; IL/OH	$14.00
Rantan Tan-Kd-Rus; Sweden	$12.00
Raola Hdw. Co.; USA	$8.00
Rattler Razor Co.; Germany	$10.00
Rawson, John; England	$10.00
Rawson & Morse; MS	$11.00
Rawson & Co.; USA	$9.00
Ray, R. "Ash Mark"; NY	$10.00
Rayson & Co.; England	$10.00
Reichard & Scheubert (R & S); NY	$9.00

Reider, Cohn Co.; MN		$11.00
Reinhard & Dinkelmann (R & D); NY		$10.00
Reio Mfg. Co.; NE		$12.00
Reliable Barber Supply; IL		$12.00
* Reliance Cut. Co.; USA		$10.00

Courtesy of Smokey Mountain Knife Works

(a) Brand and Origin Base Value	(b) Handle Material % Value	(c) Artwork % Value	(d) Condition % Value	(e) Collector Value
Reliance Cutlery Co. USA **$10.00**	Celluloid 10 x 300%= **$30.00**	Ear of corn design 10 x 250%= **$25.00**	Collectible **100%**	$30 + $25=$55 $55 x 100%= **$55.00**

Remiehneppo; Germany		$10.00
* Remington Arms Co.; USA		$28.00
Reppenhagen; NY		$10.00
Retail Cut. Assn.; NY		$12.00
Reuter Bros.; NY		$11.00
Revel, George; USA		$5.00
Revet, Richard; Germany		$7.00
Revitt; Germany		$8.00

Courtesy of Smokey Mountain Knife Works

(a) Brand and Origin Base Value	(b) Handle Material % Value	(c) Artwork % Value	(d) Condition % Value	(e) Collector Value
Remington Arms Co. USA **$28.00**	Candy Stripe Celluloid 28 x 300%= **$84.00**	Colorful interesting 28 x 200%= **$56.00**	Collectible **100%**	$84+$56=$140 $140 x 100%= **$140.00**

* Reynolds, Fredrick; England	$15.00
R.H. & Sons; England	$10.00
Rhodes & Champion; England	$10.00
Rich, R.; England	$11.00
Richard, Joseph Co.; England	$10.00

Courtesy of Smokey Mountain Knife Works

(a) Brand and Origin Base Value	(b) Handle Material % Value	(c) Artwork % Value	(d) Condition % Value	(e) Collector Value
Fredrick Reynolds England **$15.00**	Brown Jigged Bone 15 x 350%= $52.50 **$53.00**	Monkey Tail imprinted w/ patent number 15 x 100%= **$15.00**	Handle chipped Collectible- **80%**	$53 + $15=$68 $68 x 80%= $54.40 **$54.00**

Richard & Conover Hardware; MA	$11.00
Rickett, James T.; England	$9.00
Riddle Hdw.; Germany	$8.00
Ridgeway, H. & Son; England	$11.00
Rieter, F.; Germany	$10.00
Riverlin Works, MA	$11.00
Rivington Works; England	$12.00
* Rizzo, Luigi Ritz; Italy	$10.00
R.J. & Sons; England	$9.00
Rob, Carl, Schaef & Co.; Germany	$8.00
Roberie; Germany	$7.00
Roberts, R.J., Razor (Boker); USA/NY	$10.00
Roberts & Co.; England	$9.00
* Robeson Cut. Co.; USA	$25.00
Robuso (Stahlwarren Fabric); Germany	$13.00
Rodeamel-Davis Co.; England	$8.00

Courtesy of Smokey Mountain Knife Works

(a) Brand and Origin Base Value	(b) Handle Material % Value	(c) Artwork % Value	(d) Condition % Value	(e) Collector Value
Luigi Rizzo Ritz Italy **$10.00**	Black Composition 10 x 150%= **$15.00**	Photo insert 10 x 250%= **$25.00**	Initials carved in handles Collectible- 75%	$15 + $25=$40 $40 x 75%= **$30.00**

Courtesy of Smokey Mountain Knife Works

(a) Brand and Origin Base Value	(b) Handle Material % Value	(c) Artwork % Value	(d) Condition % Value	(e) Collector Value
Robeson Cut Co. USA Suredge **$25.00**	1-piece Pearl 25 x 400%= **$100.00**	Nonexistent 0	Small crack at bolster pin Collectible- 85%	$100+$0=$100 $100 x 85%= **$85.00**

Rodearmel, M.G.; England	$6.00
Roffler, Edmond; France	$12.00
Roffler Ind. Inc.; Germany	$10.00
* Rogers, Joseph & Sons; England	$19.00
Rogers, Wm.; England	$16.00
Rogers, Wm.; CT	$20.00
Rohner, L.; PA	$9.00
Rolka & Klein Co.; Germany	$7.00
Rosenbaum, Magal; Germany	$8.00
Rosenbaum, G.; Germany	$8.00
Rossler & Co.; TX	$11.00
Rotherham; Germany	$9.00
Royalty, F.W. & Co.; IL	$9.00
Royland-Widow; England	$11.00

Courtesy of Smokey Mountain Knife Works

(a) Brand and Origin Base Value	(b) Handle Material % Value	(c) Artwork % Value	(d) Condition % Value	(e) Collector Value
Joseph Rogers & Sons England **$19.00**	Horn Handles 19 x 250%= $47.50 **$48.00**	Carved handles, blade etched 19 x 300%= **$57.00**	Good **150%**	$48+$57=$105 $105 x 150%= $157.50 **$158.00**

R.S.E. Cutlery Corp; Chicago	$12.00
Ruddimann; Edinburgh, Scotland	$12.00
Ruff, G.W.; Germany	$10.00
Russell Cutlery Co., MA	$17.00
Rye, Wm.; England	$11.00
S. & A. Co. (Sperry & Alexander); NY	$10.00
Safe Razor Co.; NY	$11.00
Saffa, John; MO	$10.00
Saint, George Co.	$8.00
St. Lawrence Cut Co.; Germany	$8.00
St. Lawrence Cut Co.; St. Louis, MO	$15.00
* Salamander Works; Germany	$11.00
* Salim, Elias & Tabdoo; NY	$9.00
* Salz, Frank & Co.; Germany/NY	$9.00
Sample & Sons; NY	$10.00
Sampson & Sons; England	$10.00
Samtschnitt Eisverquiet; Germany	$9.00
Sandburg Barber Supply Co.; Germany	$9.00
Sando Cut. Co.; NY	$11.00
Sandrowitx Bro.; OH	$9.00
Sauderson Bros.; England	$10.00
Savage, G. & Sons; England	$11.00

Courtesy of the Dewey Whited Collection

(a) Brand and Origin Base Value	(b) Handle Material % Value	(c) Artwork % Value	(d) Condition % Value	(e) Collector Value
Salamander Works Germany **$11.00**	Slick Black 11 x 150%= $16.50 **$17.00**	Blade etch 11 x 200%= **$22.00**	Collectible- **80%**	$17 + $22=$39 $39 x 80%= $31.20 **$31.00**

Courtesy of Smokey Mountain Knife Works

(a) Brand and Origin Base Value	(b) Handle Material % Value	(c) Artwork % Value	(d) Condition % Value	(e) Collector Value
Salim Elias & Tabdoo New York **$9.00**	Ivory Celluloid 9 x 300%= **$27.00**	Standing nude w/ morning glory & blade etch (fancy) 9 x 550%= $49.50 **$50.00**	Good **150%**	$27 + $50=$77 $77 x 150%= $115.50 **$116.00**

Courtesy of Smokey Mountain Knife Works

(a) Brand and Origin Base Value	(b) Handle Material % Value	(c) Artwork % Value	(d) Condition % Value	(e) Collector Value
Frank Salz & Co. NY/Germany **$9.00**	Ivory Celluloid 9 x 300%= **$27.00**	Standing nude w/ rose 9 x 450%= $40.50 **$41.00**	Good **150%**	$27 + $41=$68 $68 x 150%= **$102.00**

* Saville, Gilbert Works, Ltd.; England	$11.00
Scargill, T.; England	$10.00
Schaaf & Co.; Germany	$9.00
Scharler, D.D. & Co.	$7.00
Schatt & Morgan; NY	$28.00
Scheepers, H.; Germany	$8.00
Schletter & Co.; England	$8.00
Schmactenburg Bros.; Germany	$11.00
Schmand; CA	$11.00
Schmid & Co.; MO/England	$10.00
Schmid & Son; MO	$11.00
Schmidt, Albert; Germany	$9.00
Schmidt, Rudolf; Germany	$9.00
Schnefel Bros.; England	$10.00
Schneider & Co.; IN	$9.00
Schneider & Chapman; Germany	$9.00

Courtesy of the Dewey Whited Collection

(a) Brand and Origin Base Value	(b) Handle Material % Value	(c) Artwork % Value	(d) Condition % Value	(e) Collector Value
Gilbert Saville Works, Ltd. England **$11.00**	Ivory Celluloid 11 x 300%= **$33.00**	Blade etch 11 x 100%= **$11.00**	Collectible **100%**	$33 + $11=$44 $44 x 100%= **$44.00**

Schneider & Metzger; Germany	$10.00
Schoenherr, R.; Germany	$9.00
Schofield, R.; England	$10.00
Schoolhouse; USA	$7.00
Schrade Cut Co.; CT	$18.00
Schrade-Walden; NY	$15.00
Schrick, F.; Germany	$9.00
Schulster, D.; NY	$10.00
Schulze, W.; Germany	$9.00
Schulze, P.; Germany	$9.00
Schwan, Fred; Germany	$8.00
Schwertlowen; Germany	$9.00
Scott, J.T.; England	$10.00
Scott, M.; England	$10.00
Scott, John; England	$10.00
Scotti, John; England	$11.00
* Sears Roebuck & Co.; Chicago, IL	$15.00
Sears & Sons, Henry 1865; USA	$20.00
Seebahm & Dieckstahl, Ltd.; England	$10.00
Seelbach Co. Inc.; Germany	$9.00
Seavey Hdw. Co.; IN	$10.00
Selke, M.; Waterbury, CT	$12.00
Sellers, John (signed); England/USA	$10.00
Sellers & Sons; England	$10.00

Courtesy of Smokey Mountain Knife Works

(a) Brand and Origin Base Value	(b) Handle Material % Value	(c) Artwork % Value	(d) Condition % Value	(e) Collector Value
Sears Roebuck & Co. Chicago, IL **$15.00**	Imitation Tortoise Shell 15 x 300%= **$45.00**	Beautiful handles 15 x 100%= **$15.00**	Good **150%**	$45 + $15=$60 $60 x 150%= **$90.00**

Selz, Emil; Germany	$9.00
* S & G Makhoul; OH	$9.00

Courtesy of the Dewey Whited Collection

(a) Brand and Origin Base Value	(b) Handle Material % Value	(c) Artwork % Value	(d) Condition % Value	(e) Collector Value
S & G Makhoul Ohio **$9.00**	Black Composition 9 x 150%= $13.50 **$14.00**	Nonexistent **0**	Collectible **100%**	$14 + 0=$14 $14 x 100%= **$14.00**

S & H (Smith & Hemingway); England	$10.00
Shaheen, A. & Co.; NY	$11.00
Shapleigh Hdw. Co.; St. Louis	$20.00
Sharp, W.; England	$12.00
Shave-Easy Co.; St. Louis, MO	$14.00
Shaw, John; England	$10.00
Shaw, Jas.; England	$11.00
Sheehan, C. H.; England	$9.00
* Sheffield Cut. Co.; England	$12.00
* Sheffield Steel; Germany	$12.00
Shemeld & Co.; Germany	$9.00
Shepherd, John; England	$10.00
Shepherd & Irvin; England	$16.00
Shinner; England	$10.00
Shirley, England	$10.00
Short, Thomas; England	$11.00
Shumate Cut.; St. Louis, MO	$15.00
Shure; Chicago, IL	$11.00

Courtesy of Smokey Mountain Knife Works

(a) Brand and Origin Base Value	(b) Handle Material % Value	(c) Artwork % Value	(d) Condition % Value	(e) Collector Value
Sheffield Cutlery England **$12.00**	Celluloid/ Candy Stripe 12 x 300%= **$36.00**	Handle pattern 12 x 100%= **$12.00**	Collectible **100%**	$36 + $12=$48 $48 x 100%= **$48.00**

Courtesy of Smokey Mountain Knife Works

(a) Brand and Origin Base Value	(b) Handle Material % Value	(c) Artwork % Value	(d) Condition % Value	(e) Collector Value
Sheffield Steel Germany **$12.00**	2-piece Pearl 12 x 400%= **$48.00**	Etched blade carved handles 12 x 550%= **$66.00**	Good **150%**	$48+$66=$114 $114 x 150%= **$171.00**

Siedhoff; Germany	$8.00
Silberstahl; Germany	$10.00
Silberstein, A.L.; Germany	$9.00
Silver King; USA	$10.00
Silver Steel; England	$10.00
* Simmons, E.C. Hdw.; St. Louis/Germany	$18.00
Simon & Sons; RI/Germany	$10.00
* Simon Pure Cut. Co.; Germany	$11.00
Simons Au Harve; France	$9.00
Slack & Grinold; England	$11.00
Slater Bro.; England	$10.00
Slayton Razor-Knife; Germany	$14.00
Smidt, H.J.; MI	$10.00

Courtesy of Smokey Mountain Knife Works

(a) Brand and Origin Base Value	(b) Handle Material % Value	(c) Artwork % Value	(d) Condition % Value	(e) Collector Value
E.C. Simmons Hdw. Co. St. Louis/ Germany **$18.00**	Genuine Pearl Handles 18 x 400%= **$72.00**	Keen Kutter blade etch carved handles 18 x 550%= **$99.00**	Good **150%**	$72+$99=$171 $171 x 150%= $256.50 **$257.00**

Courtesy of Smokey Mountain Knife Works

(a) Brand and Origin Base Value	(b) Handle Material % Value	(c) Artwork % Value	(d) Condition % Value	(e) Collector Value
Simon Pure Cutlery Co. Germany **$11.00**	Composition 11 x 150%= $16.50 **$17.00**	Corn design on handles 11 x 350%= $38.50 **$39.00**	Good **150%**	$17 + $39=$56 $56 x 150%= **$84.00**

Smith, Albert; NJ	$11.00
Smith Bros.; Boston/Germany	$11.00
Smith J. & Sons; England	$9.00
Smith, Thomas; MA	$11.00
Smith & Hall; England	$10.00
Smith & Hawksley; England	$10.00
Smith & Hemenway; NY	$11.00
Smith & Son, Jos.; England	$9.00
Smith & Sons, Geo.; England	$9.00
Söderein; Eskilstuna, Sweden	$11.00
Southern, Barber Sup. Co.; TX	$14.00
Southern, R.S. Co.; TX	$20.00

* Southern & Richardson; England	$11.00
Spaudling & Co.; NY	$10.00
Special; Germany	$9.00
Specialty Trading Co.; Germany	$9.00
Speed, W.H.; Germany	$10.00
Spencer & Lens Co.; England	$11.00
Spies, W.; England	$8.00
Spikusan; England	$9.00
Spokane Barber Sup.; WA	$11.00
Spot-Cash Barber Sup.; NY	$11.00
Spring; England	$10.00
Springer, G.R.; KS	$10.00
Sprock; Germany	$8.00
S.S.A.; Eskilstuna, Sweden	$12.00
S & S National Cutlery Co.; OH	$11.00
Stacey Bros.; England	$8.00
* Stader, O.; Germany	$9.00
Stadion Gold; Germany	$9.00
Stanbaugh, T.; OH	$25.00
Standard Cut. & Grinding Co.; CA	$17.00
Standart Bros.; Detroit, MI	$19.00
Stanifarth, Wm.	$9.00
Staniforth, Perkin & Co.; USA	$10.00
Staniland, R.; Germany	$8.00
Stanley, Jos.; England	$10.00
Stanter; England	$10.00
Stanton; England	$9.00
Stecher, F.W.; OH	$8.00
Steer & Webster; England	$10.00
Steinen Sup. Co.; CA	$9.00
Stephen, Karl; MA	$10.00
Stephen & Son; MA	$11.00
Sterling, Sherman & Co.; NY	$11.00
Sterling, W.; Germany	$8.00

Courtesy of Smokey Mountain Knife Works

(a) Brand and Origin Base Value	(b) Handle Material % Value	(c) Artwork % Value	(d) Condition % Value	(e) Collector Value
Southern & Richardson England **$11.00**	Slick Black Composition 11 x 150%= $16.50 **$17.00**	Blade etched 11 x 200%= **$22.00**	Good **150%**	$17 + $22=$39 $39 x 150%= $58.50 **$59.00**

Courtesy of Smokey Mountain Knife Works

(a) Brand and Origin Base Value	(b) Handle Material % Value	(c) Artwork % Value	(d) Condition % Value	(e) Collector Value
O. Stader Germany **$9.00**	Slick Black Composition 9 x 150%= $13.50 **$14.00**	Fancy handle w/ inlay of Victorian lady 9 x 400%= **$36.00**	Collectible+ **125%**	$14 + $36=$50 $50 x 125%= $62.50 **$63.00**

Sterling Co.; MD	$12.00
Sterling Mfg. Co.; USA	$12.00
Sterling Razor Works; Germany	$9.00
Stevens, Jason; England	$9.00
Stewart & Co.; England	$9.00
Stewart & Montgomery; IL	$11.00
Stockholm Razor Co.; Sweden	$10.00
Strand, A.; England	$9.00
Strass Co. B.; NY	$10.00
Straub, S. & H.; MI	$9.00
Strutz & Clotta Co.; IL	$9.00

Sunbury Barber Supply; PA	$11.00
Sunrise, Ray; USA	$11.00
Superior Razor Co.; England	$7.00
Supplee & Riddle Hdw. Co.; PA	$10.00
Sutton, W.; England	$8.00
Swain & Co. R.A.; USA	$10.00
Swan, Charles R.; Germany	$10.00
Swartz, C.W. & Co.; Germany	$9.00
Swedish Razor Co.; Sweden	$10.00
Tadross, Anton; Germany	$10.00
Taghiabge Co.; Germany	$7.00
Talbot, Brooks & Ayer; England	$9.00
* Tapross, Antoni; Germany	$9.00

Courtesy of the Dewey Whited Collection

(a) Brand and Origin Base Value	(b) Handle Material % Value	(c) Artwork % Value	(d) Condition % Value	(e) Collector Value
Antoni Tapross Germany **$9.00**	Celluloid 9 x 300%= **$27.00**	Interesting handle blade etch 9 x 300%= **$27.00**	Collectible **100%**	$27 + $27=$54 $54 x 100%= **$54.00**

Tarnow, J. Co.; Canada	$12.00
Tartter Rue Coquillere; Spain	$11.00
Taylor Bros.; England	$9.00
Taylor & Co.; England	$10.00
Taylor, G.H.; England	$10.00
Taylor, L.M.; Cincinnati, OH	$14.00
Taylor (eye) Witness; Germany	$14.00

Temer Cut. Co.; NY	$11.00
Temperite; USA	$9.00
Terrier Cut. Co., (Robeson); NY, USA	$20.00
Thibault, L.A.; MA	$10.00
Thistle Cut. Co.; NY	$18.00
Thomas Co., OH	$12.00
Thomas Mfg. Co.; Dayton, OH	$10.00
Thompson; USA	$9.00
Thurlinley & Co.	$8.00
Tillotson & Co.; England	$10.00
Tisdale, Jos.; England	$10.00
Tondeo-Werke; Germany	$10.00
Tonks, W.; England	$11.00
Tonsorial; England	$12.00
Tornblum; Sweden	$19.00
* Torrey, J.R.; Worchester, MA	$10.00

Courtesy of Smokey Mountain Knife Works

(a) Brand and Origin Base Value	(b) Handle Material % Value	(c) Artwork % Value	(d) Condition % Value	(e) Collector Value
J.R. Torrey Co. Worchester, MA **$10.00**	Imitation Tortoise Shell 10 x 300%= **$30.00**	Nonexistent **0**	Collectible **100%**	$30 + 0=$30 $30 x 100%= **$30.00**

Tower Brand; Germany	$10.00
Townley Metal & Hdw. Co.; Germany	$9.00
Tregor & Co.; Germany	$9.00
Trembley, A.A.; Canada	$11.00
Trenton Cut. Co.; USA	$14.00
Trenton Razor Co.; USA	$14.00
Trion, E.K. Co.; PA	$8.00
Tripalt Barber Supply Co.; PA	$9.00

Listings of Companies & Base Values

Tur-Edge Cut. Co.; NY	$15.00
Tryon Co., E.K.; Philadelphia, PA	$11.00
Tryon, Geo.	$9.00
T.T. Co.; Germany	$10.00
Tuck Mfg. Co.; Boston, MA	$10.00
Tuckmar; Germany	$8.00
Tudor, N.; England	$9.00
Turner & Colishaw; Meriden, CT	$11.00
Turner, I.; England	$9.00
Turner, Jos.; Sheffield	$10.00
* Turner, Thomas; England	$10.00

Courtesy of the Dewey Whited Collection

(a) Brand and Origin Base Value	(b) Handle Material % Value	(c) Artwork % Value	(d) Condition % Value	(e) Collector Value
Thomas Turner England **$10.00**	Ivory Celluloid 10 x 300%= **$30.00**	Interesting handle design 10 x 100%= **$10.00**	Collectible **100%**	$30 + $10=$40 $40 x 100%= **$40.00**

Twentieth Century Mfg. Co.; IL	$12.00
Twinplex Sales Co.; MO	$9.00
* Tyzack, J.W. Co.; England	$15.00
Ulmer; Germany	$10.00
Uncle Sam Razor; Germany	$10.00
Underland & Co.; NE	$10.00
Underwood, A.L.; NE	$10.00
Union Barber Supply; NY	$20.00
Union City; GA	$15.00

Courtesy of Smokey Mountain Knife Works

(a) Brand and Origin Base Value	(b) Handle Material % Value	(c) Artwork % Value	(d) Condition % Value	(e) Collector Value
J.W. Tyzack Co. "Railroad Arch" England **$15.00**	Pickbone 15 x 350%= $52.50 **$53.00**	Plain blade etch 15 x 125%= $18.75 **$19.00**	Good **150%**	$53 + $19=$72 $72 x 150%= **$108.00**

* Union Cut. Co.; Olean, NY	$22.00
Union Cut. Co.; NJ	$30.00
* Union Cut Co.; Little Valley, NY	$22.00
Union Razor Co.; GA	$8.00
United & B.J.S. Co.; OH	$11.00
United Drug Co.; MO	$9.00
United States Mfg. Co.; USA	$20.00
Unwin & Rogers Supply; England	$8.00
U.S. Barber Supply; TX	$11.00
U.S. Cut; St. Louis, MO	$13.00
U.S. Cut. Co.; NJ	$11.00
U.S. Cut. Mfg. Co.; Chicago	$14.00

Courtesy of the Dewey Whited Collection

(a) Brand and Origin Base Value	(b) Handle Material % Value	(c) Artwork % Value	(d) Condition % Value	(e) Collector Value
Union Cut Co. Olean, NY **$22.00**	Celluloid 22 x 300%= **$66.00**	Pretty handles but no special artwork 22 x 100%= **$22.00**	Collectible **100%**	$66 + $22=$88 $88 x 100%= **$88.00**

Courtesy of Smokey Mountain Knife Works

(a) Brand and Origin Base Value	(b) Handle Material % Value	(c) Artwork % Value	(d) Condition % Value	(e) Collector Value
Union Cutlery Co. Little Valley, NY **$22.00**	Cream Color Twist Celluloid 22 x 300%= **$66.00**	Etched blade twist handles 22 x 300%= **$66.00**	Collectible **100%**	$66+$66=$132 $132 x 100%= **$132.00**

Utica (Kut Master); NY, USA	$30.00
Utica Knife & Razor Co. (Kut Master); NY	$30.00
Valentine & Yule; IL	$10.00
Van Camp Hdw. & Iron; IN	$15.00
Van Camp Hdw. Co.; IN	$15.00
Victory Hone Co.; IA	$10.00
* Vienna; England	$10.00

Courtesy of Smokey Mountain Knife Works

(a) Brand and Origin Base Value	(b) Handle Material % Value	(c) Artwork % Value	(d) Condition % Value	(e) Collector Value
Vienna England **$10.00**	Genuine Tortoise Shell 10 x 500%= **$50.00**	Plain+ 10 x 150%= **$15.00**	Good **150%**	$50 + $15=$65 $65 x 150%= $97.50 **$98.00**

Vinnegut Hdw. Co.; IN	$11.00
Virgil, J. Revet; England	$10.00
Virginia Hdw. Co.; VA	$9.00
Vogel, E.D.; PA	$8.00

Voight Barber Supply Co.; MO	$10.00
Volart Cut. Co.; England	$8.00
Vom Cliff & Co.; NY	$12.00
Voss, Emil; Germany	$20.00
Voss Cut. Co.; NY/Germany	$18.00
Wabeek & Joseph; England	$10.00
✶ ✶ Wade & Butcher; England	$24.00
Wade, Robert; England	$11.00
Wade, Winfield & Rowbotham; England	$15.00
Wadsworth Cut. Co.; Germany	$10.00

Courtesy of Smokey Mountain Knife Works

(a) Brand and Origin Base Value	(b) Handle Material % Value	(c) Artwork % Value	(d) Condition % Value	(e) Collector Value
Wade & Butcher England **$24.00**	Iridescent Pearl Handles 24 x 400%= **$96.00**	Carved handles 24 x 350%= **$84.00**	Cracked handle at pin Collectible- **80%**	$96+$84=$180 $180 x 80%= **$144.00**

Courtesy of Smokey Mountain Knife Works

(a) Brand and Origin Base Value	(b) Handle Material % Value	(c) Artwork % Value	(d) Condition % Value	(e) Collector Value
Wade & Butcher England **$24.00**	Genuine 3- piece Pearl Handles 24 x 400%= **$96.00**	Nickel silver bolsters 24 x 250%= **$60.00**	Major crack & stain Collectible- **60%**	$96+$60=$156 $156 x 60%= $93.60 **$94.00**

* Wadsworth & Sons; Germany		$9.00
Wagner, Wilhelm; Germany		$12.00
Walker, D.N.; Washington, D.C.		$12.00
Walker & Gibson; Germany		$10.00
Walker & Hall; England		$12.00
Walker Hardware Co.; USA		$11.00
Wall Bros.; England		$10.00
Wallace, Fred; England		$9.00
Walter, J. & Son; England		$10.00
Walter, R.E. & Son; England		$11.00
Walter, T.; England		$11.00
Walter, W.; England		$10.00
Walter's Sons, W. & B.; England		$10.00
Walterino, J.; England		$10.00
Wapenhutchers; England		$9.00
Warburton, Samuel; England		$11.00
Warburton, T.; England		$10.00
Ward Bros.; England		$10.00
Warranted; Gate City, TN, USA		$17.00
Warren, J.M. & Co.; NY		$10.00
Warren Bros.; England		$9.00
Warren Pearl Works; PA		$11.00
Warren, Hart & Leslie; England		$9.00

Courtesy of Smokey Mountain Knife Works

(a) Brand and Origin Base Value	(b) Handle Material % Value	(c) Artwork % Value	(d) Condition % Value	(e) Collector Value
Wadsworth Razor Co. Germany **$9.00**	Celluloid 9 x 300%= **$27.00**	Fancy inlay floral design on handles 9 x 400%= **$36.00**	Collectible **100%**	$27 + $36=$63 $63 x 100%= **$63.00**

Washington Cutlery Co.; Germany/USA	$10.00
Washington Cutlery Co.; WI	$10.00
Washington Dry Goods; Germany	$10.00
Wassermann, E.; OH	$10.00
Waterville Cutlery Co.; CT	$32.00
Waterville Mfg. Co.; CT	$36.00
Wayne Cutlery Co.; NY	$11.00
Weck, Ed & Sons; NY	$9.00
Wedge	$9.00
Weeden-Kremp; Il	$10.00
Weiden, Mill; Germany	$9.00
Weigelt, A.; Germany	$9.00
Weiner, S.; Germany	$8.00
* Weis, J.H. Supply House; Louisville, KY	$15.00
Weiss & Stapek; Germany	$10.00
Welkert, C.; PA	$9.00
Well & Clement; OH	$10.00
Wells, B.B.; England	$10.00
Wells, M.; England	$10.00
Wells, A. Mellegar	$8.00
Weske Cutlery Co.; OH	$11.00
West; England	$8.00

Courtesy of Smokey Mountain Knife Works

(a) Brand and Origin Base Value	(b) Handle Material % Value	(c) Artwork % Value	(d) Condition % Value	(e) Collector Value
J. H. Weis Supply House Louisville, KY **$15.00**	Genuine Pearl Handles 15 x 400%= **$60.00**	22 bullet inlay 15 x 300%= **$45.00**	Good **150%**	$60+$45=$105 $105 x 150%= $157.50 **$158.00**

Listings of Companies & Base Values

West Point; USA		$10.00
Wester Bros.; Germany		$10.00
* Wester Bros.; NY		$12.00

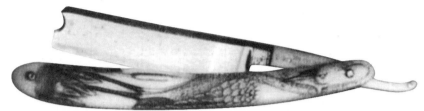

Courtesy of Smokey Mountain Knife Works

(a) Brand and Origin Base Value	(b) Handle Material % Value	(c) Artwork % Value	(d) Condition % Value	(e) Collector Value
Wester Bros. NY **$12.00**	Red Celluloid 12 x 300%= **$36.00**	Relief crane with fish in mouth 12 x 400%= **$48.00**	Good **150%**	$36 + $48=$84 $84 x 150%= **$126.00**

Wester Stone & Co.; Germany	$15.00
Western Barber Supply Co.; PA	$10.00
Western Cutlery Co. (W & H); Germany	$11.00
Western States Cutlery Co.; CO	$24.00
Westerfield Mfg. Co.; Germany	$9.00
Westhoff & Co.; CA	$10.00
Westpfal, Davis & Co.; Germany	$8.00
Westpfal, F. & Bros.; Germany	$9.00
Westpfal, Fred; Germany	$9.00
Westpfal, Paul; NY	$11.00
Weyer, G.H.; MO/Germany	$10.00
Weyerberg, Goggfried & Sohn; Germany	$10.00
Whatham, Thomas & Co.; England	$11.00
Wheeldon; England	$8.00
Whitehead, W & H; England	$11.00
Whitney, R.H. & Co.; USA	$10.00
Wiebusch & Hilger; NY	$11.00
Wiesenfeld; IL/England	$10.00

Wilbert, (ELK); Chicago/Germany	$12.00
Wilkins, H.; England	$11.00
Will & Finch; San Francisco, CA/Germany	$12.00
William, A.; USA	$9.00
Willis, G.; USA	$10.00
Wilson & Bros. Co.; England	$10.00
Wilson, W. & Son; England	$10.00
Wilson & Southern; England	$10.00
Wilson & Swift; England	$10.00
Wilson, Hawksworth & Moss; England	$11.00
Wilton, J.; England	$10.00
* Wilton, W.D.; England	$11.00

Courtesy of Smokey Mountain Knife Works

(a) Brand and Origin Base Value	(b) Handle Material % Value	(c) Artwork % Value	(d) Condition % Value	(e) Collector Value
W. D. Wilton Celebrated Razor England **$11.00**	Horn 11 x 200%= **$22.00**	Pressed motif floral design 11 x 400%= **$44.00**	Good **150%**	$22 + $44=$66 $66 x 150%= **$99.00**

Winchester Trademark; CT	$45.00
Windler, H.; Germany	$9.00
Wingen, A.; Germany	$14.00
Wingfield & Rowbotham Co.; England	$11.00
Wilkinson Sword; England	$25.00
Winks & Sons; England	$10.00
Wiss, Jacob & Son; NJ/Germany	$10.00
Withers, Benjamin & Co.; IL	$10.00
Witte Cut. Co.; Germany	$9.00
Witte Hardware Co.; Germany	$9.00

Wohfer, C.; PA	$10.00
Wolfe (Crown), J. Sheperd Werks	$11.00
Wolfe, C.; MI	$10.00
Wolfertz & Co.; CA/PA	$10.00
Wolff, Lane & Co.; Germany	$9.00
Wood, Bickmail & Potter; England	$7.00
Woodbury, John	$10.00
Woodhead, G.; England	$14.00
Wood Work & Co. F.H.; Chattanooga, TN	$14.00
Worchester Razor Co.; MA	$12.00
Worral, G.; England	$10.00
Worth, B & Sons; England	$11.00
Worthington, George Co.; Cleveland, OH	$12.00
* Wostenholm, George (IXL); England	$16.00

Courtesy of Smokey Mountain Knife Works

(a) Brand and Origin Base Value	(b) Handle Material % Value	(c) Artwork % Value	(d) Condition % Value	(e) Collector Value
George Wostenholm England **$16.00**	2-piece Pearl 16 x 400%= **$64.00**	Silver bar inlay grooved handles 16 x 400%= **$64.00**	Good **150%**	$64+$64=$128 $128 x 150%= **$192.00**

Wragg, John & Son; England	$20.00
Wright, Wm, J. & R.; England	$10.00
Wright & Wilhelmy Co.; Germany	$8.00
W. X. Y. & Z. Cutlery Co.; England	$9.00
Wysard, The, Co.; PA	$9.00
* Yankee Cutlery Co.; Germany	$11.00
Yazbek, Lahod; OH	$9.00
York Cut Co.	$10.00

York, Wadsworth & Co.; England		$11.00
Youngstown Barber Supply; OH		$12.00
Zacour Bros.; Germany		$8.00
Zaloom, Malouf & Co.; Germany		$7.00
Zartina Cutlery Works; Germany		$11.00
* Zepp; Germany		$7.00

Courtesy of Smokey Mountain Knife Works

(a) Brand and Origin Base Value	(b) Handle Material % Value	(c) Artwork % Value	(d) Condition % Value	(e) Collector Value
Yankee Cutlery "Lion Brand" Germany **$11.00**	Ivory Celluloid 11 x 300%= **$33.00**	Blade etch floral motif 11 x 300%= **$33.00**	Collectible **100%**	$33 + $33=$66 $66 x 100%= **$66.00**

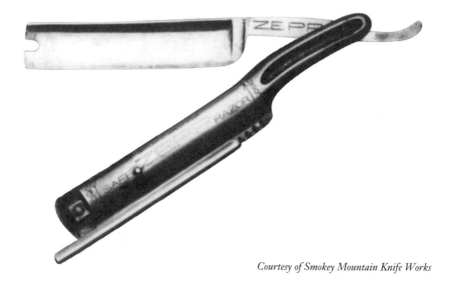

Courtesy of Smokey Mountain Knife Works

(a) Brand and Origin Base Value	(b) Handle Material % Value	(c) Artwork % Value	(d) Condition % Value	(e) Collector Value
Zepp **$7.00**	Aluminum 7 x 350%= $24.50 **$25.00**	Interesting design 7 x 100%= **$7.00**	Collectible **100%**	$25 + $7=$32 $32 x 100%= **$32.00**

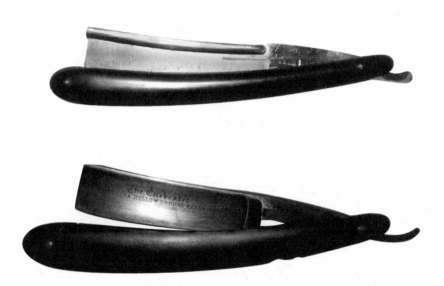

Courtesy of Smokey Mountain Knife Works

The giant meat chopper razor is among the earliest of the straight razors. It will bring about four to five times the value of a comparable straight razor, by the same company, with the same handle material as a later model.

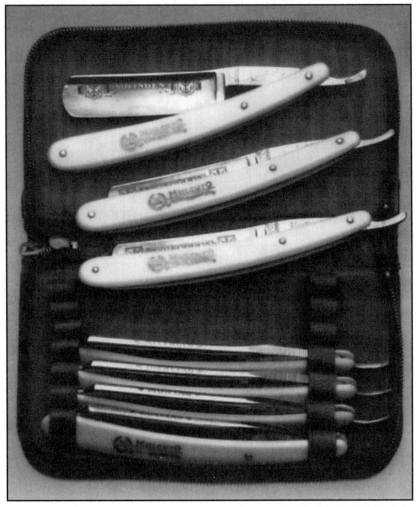

Courtesy of Smokey Mountain Knife Works

A seven day set of razors, such as this German-made set by Mukoto, in the original box, should be valued about 10 times the price of a single razor of comparable brand, handle material, artwork, and condition.

Courtesy of Smokey Mountain Knife Works

These old boys are probably among the earliest of folding straights. They have no brand stamp. Can you imagine pulling one of these across your face some morning? Talk about removing hide, hair, and all!

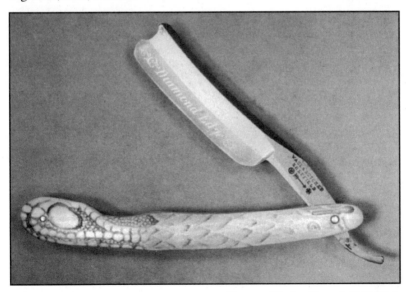

Courtesy of Smokey Mountain Knife Works

This carved, genuine ivory handled, Wade & Butcher Diamond Edge is an excellent example of how outstanding razor art can be.

When displaying a collection or a single item, a collector will find that related/supportive items will both add interest and enhance the value of the collectible. Straight razors are no exception to this observation.

Even though we've made no attempt to calculate the value of the following items, we felt you might want to picture them with your collection.

We suggest that you should always be on the lookout for reasonably priced related barber and shaving items to include in your collection.

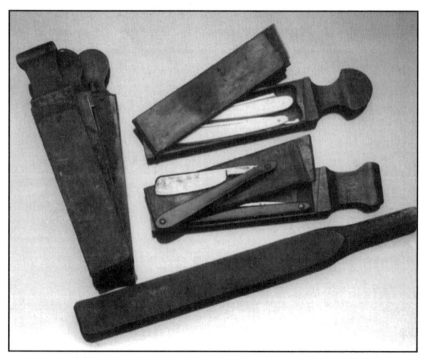

Courtesy of Smokey Mountain Knife Works

Courtesy of Smokey Mountain Knife Works

Courtesy of Smokey Mountain Knife Works

Razor Hones.

Courtesy of Smokey Mountain Knife Works

Shaving mirror with drawer.

Courtesy of Smokey Mountain Knife Works

Hair Tonic Sign.

Courtesy of Smokey Mountain Knife Works

Winchester/Simmons Shaving Mirror.

Courtesy of Smokey Mountain Knife Works

Table Top Shaving Mirrors.

Grandpaw's razor can rarely be purchased at market value. Always get grandson to price it first, if he wishes to sell it. Otherwise you'll probably insult him. Heirlooms probably should remain at home. You just can't pay for family history. The razors pictured above belonged to the authors' grandfathers, Cicero Langdon and Jable Stewart. Even though they aren't particularly valuable, they do not have a price.

Author's Collection

Author's Collection

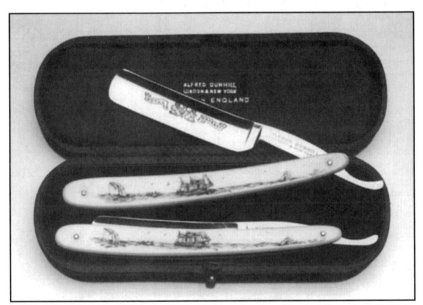

Courtesy of Smokey Mountain Knife Works

A pair of razors, in their original box, certainly make a handsome display. The collector should expect to pay about three times the price of an individual razor from the same company with similar appointments and condition. Shown is a set of Alfred Dunhill razors with scrimshawed, genuine ivory handles.

Courtesy of Smokey Mountain Knife Works

The original box, in good condition, can add as much as 10% to the value of a razor.